AMERICA IN TWO CENTURIES:
An Inventory

AMERICA IN TWO CENTURIES:
An Inventory

Advisory Editor

DANIEL J. BOORSTIN

*See last pages of this volume
for a complete list of titles*

NATIONAL INCOME
IN THE UNITED STATES
1799–1938

ROBERT F. MARTIN

ARNO PRESS
A New York Times Company
1976

791979

Editorial Supervision: ANDREA HICKS

———··⟨∞⟩··———

Reprint Edition 1976 by Arno Press Inc.

Reprinted from a copy in
  The Newark Public Library

AMERICA IN TWO CENTURIES: An Inventory
ISBN for complete set: 0-405-07666-6
See last pages of this volume for titles.

Manufactured in the United States of America

———··⟨∞⟩··———

Library of Congress Cataloging in Publication Data

National Industrial Conference Board.
    National income in the United States, 1799-1938.

    (America in two centuries an inventory)
    Reprint of the 1939 ed. published by the National
Industrial Conference Board, New York, which was
issued as no. 241 of National Industrial Conference
Board studies.
    1. National income--United States--History. 2. U-
nited States--Economic conditions. I. Martin,
Robert Fitz-Randolph, 1900-   II. Title.   III. Se-
ries.   IV. Series: National Industrial Conference
Board. Studies ; no. 241.
HC110.I5N38 1976   339.2'0973   75-22827

ISBN 0-405-07699-1

NATIONAL INCOME
IN THE UNITED STATES
1799-1938

NATIONAL INDUSTRIAL CONFERENCE BOARD STUDIES
NUMBER 241

NATIONAL INCOME IN THE UNITED STATES 1799–1938

By

ROBERT F. MARTIN, *Director*

Economic Research Division, THE CONFERENCE BOARD

ORGANIZED 1916

NATIONAL INDUSTRIAL CONFERENCE BOARD, Inc.

247 PARK AVENUE

NEW YORK CITY

January, 1939
241

FOREWORD

THIS publication presents the latest of the studies in the field of income that have been produced by the Conference Board's economic research staff in recent years.[1] The purpose of these studies is to add to the existing body of information regarding the amount, history, composition and distribution of the national income, to improve and clarify the technique of estimating it, and to promote better understanding of the interpretation and proper application of national income estimates among the business community and the general public who are now accustomed to attach great importance to them because of their common use for political as well as practical business purposes.

This study offers the most complete estimates of national income in the United States that are available for the 140-year period beginning in 1799. The sources and methods used in constructing them are fully explained in the Appendix. Though in the nature of such estimates they are not comprehensive and perfect, they are the best approximations possible in the present state of our information in this field, and they present in the most compact form a composite picture of America's economic development such as no other series

[1] These include the following books and articles:
Books:
"Income Received in the Various States," 1937
"Income in Agriculture, 1929–1935," 1936
"National Income and Its Elements," 1936

Conference Board Bulletin articles:
"The National Income in 1936 and 1937," February, 1938
"Income Received in the Various States in 1936 and 1937," February, 1938
"Realized National Income, 1909–1935," April, 1937
"Income from the Fuel and Power Industries," December, 1937
"Income from Bituminous Coal Mining," March, 1937
"Redistribution of Income," December, 1936
"Income from Transportation, 1929–1935," October, 1936
"Income from Manufacturing, 1929–1935," July, 1936

of statistics can. Many different interpretations of this picture are undoubtedly possible, and Dr. Martin, who has been sufficiently preoccupied with the difficult task of compiling the data and constructing the estimates, has ventured only to indicate those interpretations which are obvious and helpful in understanding the figures. What light this record throws on some of the problems of the present he—and the Conference Board—prefer to leave the reader to judge for himself.

In the preparation of this study Dr. Martin makes grateful acknowledgment of the assistance of Mr. Harlow D. Osborne, principal assistant in charge of the statistical work, and Miss Marie L. La Branche, of the Conference Board's research staff, and of the fine encouragement and direct assistance rendered by Dr. Willford I. King, of New York University, in making his own estimate worksheets and experienced observations freely available throughout the progress of the work.

VIRGIL JORDAN
President

New York City
January, 1939

CONTENTS

LIST OF TABLES

LIST OF CHARTS

SUMMARY

DURING the past 140 years the income received by individuals in the United States has increased from less than $1 billion to a peak of almost $80 billion in 1929 and a level of $69 billion in 1937.[1] Part of the fluctuations in income have been caused by changing price levels, but even after adjustment for changes in this factor the realized national income has multiplied about seventy times between 1799 and 1937.

Taking into account the increase in population in the United States as well as the changing price level it is found that the per capita real income, or income in terms of goods and services purchasable with the dollars received, has increased nearly three-fold between 1799 and 1937.

Another striking fact brought out by the per capita real income data is the irregularity of economic advancement throughout the history of the United States. The best available data indicate an actual decline in the economic well-being of individuals during the disturbed period of American history in which the War of 1812 and the later Indian Wars occurred. After a very rapid advance in the 1840's and 1850's there was again a set-back consequent upon the Civil War. Thereafter a period of rapid expansion set in which was checked only by the post-World War depressions.

Miscellaneous Income Items

That part of the total realized national income which is derived from sources not directly related to current organized production has been rising in importance, particularly in recent years. Pensions and compensation for injuries, relief payments, rent on homes and interest on mortgages on homes,

---

[1] A preliminary estimate for 1938 is $62 billion. See Chapter I.

as well as direct government subsidies to farmers, have been accounting for a larger portion of the national income total. In 1937 these items amounted to $6.5 billion in the total of $69 billion or about 10%, whereas in 1799 these items accounted for only $3 million of the total realized income of $677 million or less than 0.5%.

Importance of Government

The importance of government as a direct source of income of individuals has also been increasing over the years. In 1799 the population looked to government for only 1% of its personal income. This proportion has been rising, with particularly striking increases during and after each war, so that by 1929 it had reached 8.6%. In the subsequent years of depression there was an unprecedented rise in the importance of government to a peak of 20% in 1936. In the latter year government thus was the immediate source of one-fifth of the income received by individuals in the United States.

Kinds of Private Production Income

Data are available showing the types of income received from private production sources annually since 1899. The progress of incorporation of business enterprises and a shifting in the importance of some industries are reflected in these figures. Salaries and wages and dividends have increased in relative importance while entrepreneurial income, interest, net rents and royalties have declined. During the 38-year period ending in 1937, salaries and wages have increased in importance from 58% to 68% of the total. The greater part of this increase occurred shortly after the World War and there has been remarkably little variation in this percentage since 1920.

Interest has declined in relative importance between 1899 and 1937, falling from 4.5% to 2.2%. It reached a high point of 6% of the total, however, during the depression subsequent to 1929, for it is a stable kind of income and held up relatively well when other kinds of income were drastically declining. Similarly, it declined rapidly in relative importance as total income recovered. Government action to reduce interest rates was also an important factor in the later years.

Entrepreneurial income, or the profits received by individual enterprisers, has declined in relative importance from 29% to 20% in the 38-year period. Meanwhile, net rents and royalties have declined from an importance of 2.8% to 1.7% and dividends have increased from 6% to 8%.

Industrial Sources of Private Production Income

The dynamic nature of the economy in the United States is well illustrated in the remarkable adjustments which have occurred in the relative position of the various industries as contributors to the national income since 1799. In that early year agriculture accounted for almost 40%, and transportation and communication for nearly 25%, of total private production income. Agriculture and its dependent industries accounted for well over two-thirds of the total income in that period. Manufacturing was of minor importance.

In 1937 manufacturing was the outstanding major source of income, accounting for nearly a third of the total. Agriculture and transportation had declined to a position of a little over 10% each, and were both exceeded in importance as a source of income by trade and by service, as well as by manufacturing. These shifts in relative importance have not occurred uniformly over the years but have taken place primarily in several dynamic periods. Details relating to these changes and to the importance of the various kinds of income in each industry will be found in Chapter III.

NATIONAL INCOME IN THE UNITED STATES 1799–1938

CHAPTER I

THE NATIONAL INCOME TOTALS

LIKE most economic statistics, national income estimates are figures with two faces. On one side they represent a composite picture of the actual goods and services that the people of the country have gotten in a given period for their consumption or for use in other ways. On the other side they represent a composite account of the cost in money of producing these goods and services. Neither of these pictures is ever complete. In both, the elements included may differ according to the purposes for which they are computed or used, or because the available information is insufficient.[1]

In any sense, however, national income estimates when constructed on a fairly comparable basis for a period of years provide a composite record of the economic activity of a country that affords a broader view and better understanding of its economic history than any other series of general statistics. For such a purpose the national income estimates presented in this book are particularly useful, since they cover over a century and a third of the growth of our national economy.

While national income estimates for early years can at best

---

[1] For a discussion of the meaning of national income estimates, the various types and the methods of compiling them, see Robert F. Martin, "National Income and Its Elements," National Industrial Conference Board, New York, 1936.

1

be only approximate, by confining them to the census years it has been possible to obtain useful results for this period. For some of the early estimates it was necessary to use figures relating to a twelve-month period not precisely within the calendar year. (For details, see Appendix.) The data here shown are derived from a more intensive examination of original documents and subsidiary sources than has heretofore been undertaken. The estimates are more reliable for the recent periods, of course, because more comprehensive source material is available.

Total Realized National Income, 1799–1938

Viewing the broad upsurge of the national income in the United States since Colonial times, the first impression is one of accelerating speed. This is true, also, of the growth in population. Chart 1, in which the rise in the national income is compared with the increase in population, shows the parallel. It is obvious that over the period as a whole a tremendous growth in population has accompanied the expansion of the national income, but the latter has been greater.

The national income is necessarily measured in dollars. Over the years, however, the quantity of goods and services which a dollar will purchase has varied greatly as their prices have changed. In Chart 2 the growth of the national income in the United States since 1799 is presented, along with an index showing roughly the rises and falls in the general price level or purchasing power of the dollar.

If the national income is to be viewed as a measure of the economic welfare of the people, it is necessary to adjust this measure both for the increase in the population and the variation in prices, or the quantity of goods and services represented by each dollar. These adjustments have been made in Chart 3, which shows the per capita national income for each year in terms of dollars of 1926 purchasing power.

At once a very striking fact appears. Over the century

CHART 1: TOTAL REALIZED INCOME (UNADJUSTED FOR PRICE CHANGES) AND POPULATION, 1799-1937

Index Numbers, 1799 = 100

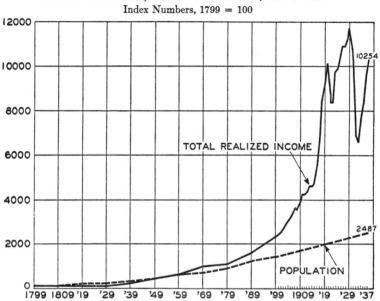

CHART 2: TOTAL REALIZED INCOME AND THE GENERAL PRICE LEVEL, 1799-1937

Index Numbers, 1926 = 100

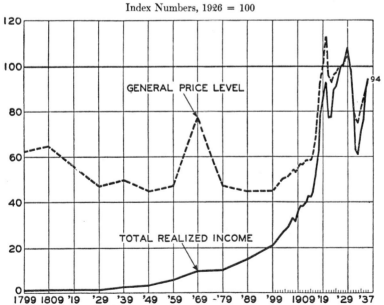

and a third covered the "real income," or quantity of goods and services represented by the dollar income of each individual in the country, has risen remarkably, from $214 per person in 1799 to $602 per person in 1937.[1] This three-fold increase represents broadly the economic advancement of the people over the whole period. To some extent, of course,

CHART 3: REALIZED NATIONAL INCOME PER CAPITA OF POPULATION, 1799–1937

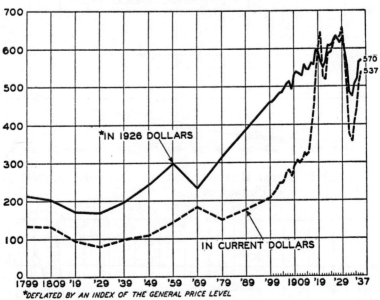

the increase in the actual volume of goods and services consumed by each individual is somewhat overstated, for in the early days a great many services were performed and goods produced within the family at home and did not therefore enter into the exchange economy and appear in the national income accounts. They were not sold for money, and the cost of their production was the labor of the individual or

[1] A preliminary estimate for 1938 indicates a reduction of this total to about $555.

the family and not a cash expenditure. The increase shown is, therefore, partly attributable to the transfer to the market of services formerly performed at home. Such specialization itself marks an important advance, however, for well-being consists of much more than the quantity of goods and services here measured. Even though the amount of goods and services that were available may not have increased as much as these estimates indicate, their variety and quality are greater, and the labor of producing them is less.

Part of the economic advance during the past century and a third has been realized in the form of shorter hours of work and in the decrease and lightening of the most burdensome tasks. This development has been particularly rapid in the later part of the period. Not only has the weekly average of full-time employment in manufacturing, for example, decreased from 59.0 hours in 1900 to 48.6 hours in 1930,[1] but heavy manual labor has been obviated or diminished by mechanized agricultural implements, motorized equipment, welding and riveting machines, and the standardization of parts. In this recent period there has also been a great improvement in the quality of products, agricultural as well as industrial, while prices have not risen correspondingly and in many cases have actually declined as a result of more efficient methods of production.

Another striking fact brought out by the data on per capita real income is that the growth in amount of goods and services produced and consumed by the individual has not been continuous. During the unsettled years after the Revolution and through the War of 1812 and the Indian Wars, there was a distinct decline in the volume of goods and services circulating per capita. Again, after the Civil War, there was another period of economic disruption, during which the eco-

---

[1] Paul H. Douglas, "Real Wages in the United States," Cambridge, Mass., 1930, p. 116; and Carroll R. Daugherty, "Labor Problems in American Industry," Cambridge, Mass., 1936, p. 242.

TABLE 1: REALIZED NATIONAL INCOME, TOTAL AND PER CAPITA, IN CURRENT DOLLARS AND CONSTANT DOLLARS OF 1926 PURCHASING POWER, 1799–1938

	Total Realized National Income						Per Capita Realized National Income					
	Millions of Dollars			Indexes, 1929 = 100			Dollars			Indexes, 1929 = 100		
Year	Current Income	Income Adjusted by the Cost of Living[1]	Income Adjusted by the General Price Level[2]	Current Income	Income Adjusted by the Cost of Living[1]	Income Adjusted by the General Price Level[2]	Current Income	Income Adjusted by the Cost of Living[1]	Income Adjusted by the General Price Level[2]	Current Income	Income Adjusted by the Cost of Living[1]	Income Adjusted by the General Price Level[2]
1799	677	1,115	1,092	0.9	1.3	1.4	131	216	211	20.0	31.7	33.8
1809	915	1,441	1,423	1.2	1.7	1.9	130	204	202	19.9	30.0	32.3
1819	876	1,625	1,576	1.1	2.0	2.1	93	173	168	14.2	25.4	26.9
1829	975	2,057	2,083	1.2	2.5	2.7	78	164	166	11.9	24.1	26.6
1839	1,631	3,295	3,282	2.1	4.0	4.3	98	198	197	15.0	29.1	31.5
1849	2,420	5,319	5,450	3.0	6.4	7.2	107	235	241	16.4	34.5	38.6
1859	4,311	9,095	9,212	5.4	11.0	12.1	140	296	300	21.4	43.5	48.0
1869	6,887	8,995	8,843	8.6	10.9	11.6	180	237	233	27.5	34.8	37.3
1879	7,227	15,183	15,442	9.1	18.3	20.3	147	309	315	22.5	45.4	50.4
1889	10,701	23,675	23,780	13.5	28.6	31.3	173	383	385	26.5	56.2	61.6
1899	15,364	36,066	34,142	19.3	43.6	45.0	205	482	456	31.3	70.8	73.0
1900	16,158	36,557	34,974	20.3	44.1	46.1	212	480	459	32.4	70.5	73.4
1901	17,170	37,903	36,224	21.6	45.8	47.7	221	488	466	33.8	71.7	74.6
1902	18,444	39,750	37,564	23.2	48.0	49.5	232	501	473	35.5	73.6	75.7
1903	19,595	40,319	38,956	24.6	48.7	51.3	242	498	481	37.0	73.1	77.0
1904	20,090	41,767	39,940	25.3	50.4	52.6	243	506	484	37.2	74.3	77.4
1905	21,428	44,549	41,608	27.0	53.8	54.8	254	529	494	38.8	77.7	79.0
1906	23,165	46,610	43,543	29.1	56.3	57.3	270	543	507	41.3	79.7	81.1
1907	24,403	46,482	44,858	30.7	56.1	59.1	279	531	513	42.7	78.0	82.1
1908	23,468	46,636	44,094	29.5	56.3	58.1	263	524	495	40.2	76.9	79.2
1909	26,456	52,596	48,102	33.3	63.5	63.4	292	580	530	44.6	85.2	84.8

Year												
1910	28,166	53,043	49,675	35.4	64.1	65.4	305	575	538	46.6	84.4	86.1
1911	28,104	52,927	50,096	35.4	63.9	66.0	300	565	535	45.9	83.0	85.6
1912	29,422	52,167	50,294	37.0	63.0	66.2	309	549	529	47.2	80.6	84.6
1913	31,450	56,872	53,761	39.6	68.7	70.8	326	589	557	49.8	86.5	89.1
1914	31,213	55,342	53,356	39.3	66.8	70.3	319	565	545	48.8	83.0	87.2
1915	32,533	57,176	54,042	40.9	69.0	71.2	327	576	544	50.0	84.6	87.0
1916	38,739	63,196	56,636	48.7	76.3	74.6	384	627	562	58.7	92.1	89.9
1917	46,376	65,595	57,043	58.3	79.2	75.1	454	642	558	69.4	94.3	89.3
1918	56,956	66,928	62,044	71.6	80.8	81.7	550	646	599	84.1	94.9	95.8
1919	62,945	65,093	62,199	79.2	78.6	81.9	599	620	592	91.6	91.0	94.7
1920	68,434	60,401	60,615	86.1	72.9	79.8	642	567	569	98.2	83.3	91.0
1921	56,689	57,787	59,485	71.3	69.8	78.3	524	534	550	80.1	78.4	88.0
1922	57,171	61,211	61,873	71.9	73.9	81.5	520	557	563	79.5	81.8	90.1
1923	65,662	68,469	68,044	82.6	82.7	89.6	589	614	610	90.1	90.2	97.6
1924	67,003	69,004	69,004	84.3	83.3	90.9	592	610	610	90.5	89.6	97.6
1925	70,051	70,474	70,474	88.1	85.1	92.8	610	614	614	93.3	90.2	98.2
1926	73,523	73,523	73,523	92.5	88.8	96.8	631	631	631	96.5	92.7	101.0
1927	73,966	75,630	73,966	93.0	91.3	97.4	626	640	626	95.7	94.0	100.2
1928	75,904	78,657	73,765	95.5	95.0	97.1	633	656	615	96.8	96.3	100.4
1929	79,498	82,810	75,929	100.0	100.0	100.0	654	681	625	100.0	100.0	100.0
1930	72,398	78,099	73,725	91.1	94.3	97.1	588	634	599	89.9	93.1	95.8
1931	60,203	72,013	68,647	75.7	87.0	90.4	485	580	553	74.2	85.2	88.5
1932	46,708	62,527	60,503	58.8	75.5	79.7	374	500	484	57.2	73.4	77.4
1933	44,713	62,274	59,301	56.2	75.2	78.1	356	495	472	54.4	72.7	75.5
1934	51,560	67,753	64,370	64.9	81.8	84.8	407	535	508	62.2	78.6	81.3
1935	56,254	71,028	66,337	70.8	85.8	87.4	441	557	520	67.4	81.8	83.2
1936	65,246	80,253	72,415	82.1	96.9	95.4	508	625	564	77.7	91.8	90.2
1937	69,419	81,766	73,693	87.3	98.7	97.1	537	633	570	82.1	93.0	91.2
1938³	62,286	75,225	69,130	78.3	90.8	91.0	478	577	531	73.1	84.7	85.0

1 Cost of Living Index, Federal Reserve Bank of New York and National Industrial Conference Board.
2 Price Index, Snyder Index, Federal Reserve Bank of New York and National Industrial Conference Board.
3 Preliminary estimate.

nomic well-being of the individual in the United States declined. There followed a period of exceptionally rapid expansion, which lasted over fifty years, and which was only terminated by a major set-back consequent upon another great war. A more intensive examination of these periods follows.

Caution must be exercised in comparing changes in national income from one decennial census period to another, for frequently the census year falls in a period of deep depression or of exceptional prosperity; and the reports are therefore liable to understate or overemphasize the actual trend of the change over the period in which the census years fall. This factor is not so important, however, when several decades are considered together. This discussion will deal first with the general trends over the longer periods, and then indicate the state of business conditions in each of the years covered by the data, as an aid in judging the significance of the less reliable indications of short-term changes.

Long-Term Trends, 1799–1849

A comparison of the per capita realized income figures, whether in terms of current dollars or dollars of constant purchasing power, as shown in Chart 3, indicates that very little actual economic advance per capita appeared in the first half of the nineteenth century. This was a period of general pioneering turmoil, punctuated by controversies, first with European countries, culminating in the War of 1812 with the British, and then the series of Black Hawk, Seminole and other Indian Wars.

Although 1849 marks the first year covered by these data in which there occurred a prosperity peak in the business cycle, nevertheless income in current dollars per capita was below that for 1799, and on an adjusted basis only between 8% and 15% above it. With such a slight increase in a year of prosperity, it is evident that the actual increase in the well-being of the population in the United States in the first half of the nineteenth century could have been only moderate.

Of course the country was developing rapidly in this period; the total realized national income quadrupled in terms of current dollars and trebled on the adjusted basis. This expansion reflected the influx of population, the use of new land and the development of agriculture and local industries. The population increased 338% in this period. Nevertheless, the advancement in the current economic welfare of individuals in this half-century was much less than has customarily been assumed.

The Census Years from 1799 to 1849

The following conditions characterized the state of business activity in the census years to which the national income estimates for the first half of the nineteenth century relate:[1]

The year 1799 was passed during a revival from depression and was a year of relative prosperity. Prices were high, foreign trade had recovered, money was easy, and industrial activity was marked. The situation was marred only by a poor harvest.

Income per capita declined slightly in terms of current dollars, and by some 5% on the adjusted basis, between 1799 and 1809. The latter year, in fact, came in a period of depression, with wide-spread business failures, tight money and a bank crisis in New England. This situation, coupled with embargoes on trade with England and France through a good part of the year, caused wide-spread business distress. Commodity prices were improving, however, and crops were fair.

A further decline in per capita income took place between 1809 and 1819. The latter year included a severe depression and a financial panic. Business activity stagnated, and speculative purchases of public land in the spring were followed

[1] For further details see Willard L. Thorp and Wesley C. Mitchell, "Business Annals," National Bureau of Economic Research, New York, 1926, Chapter I.

TABLE 2: REALIZED PRODUCTION INCOME, TOTAL AND PER CAPITA, IN CURRENT DOLLARS AND CONSTANT DOLLARS OF 1926 PURCHASING POWER, 1799–1938

Year	Total Realized Production Income						Per Capita Realized Production Income					
	Current Income	Income Adjusted by the Cost of Living[1]	Income Adjusted by the General Price Level[2]	Current Income	Income Adjusted by the Cost of Living[1]	Income Adjusted by the General Price Level[2]	Current Income	Income Adjusted by the Cost of Living[1]	Income Adjusted by the General Price Level[2]	Current Income	Income Adjusted by the Cost of Living[1]	Income Adjusted by the General Price Level[2]
	Millions of Dollars			Indexes, 1929 = 100			Dollars			Indexes, 1929 = 100		
1799	674	1,110	1,087	0.9	1.4	1.5	130	215	210	21.0	33.4	35.6
1809	912	1,436	1,418	1.2	1.8	2.0	129	204	201	20.9	31.7	34.1
1819	870	1,614	1,565	1.2	2.1	2.2	93	172	167	15.0	26.7	28.3
1829	967	2,040	2,066	1.3	2.6	2.9	77	163	165	12.5	25.3	28.0
1839	1,614	3,261	3,247	2.2	4.2	4.5	97	196	195	15.7	30.5	33.1
1849	2,383	5,237	5,367	3.2	6.7	7.5	105	231	237	17.0	35.9	40.2
1859	4,198	8,857	8,970	5.6	11.3	12.5	137	289	292	22.2	44.9	49.5
1869	6,559	8,642	8,496	8.7	11.1	11.8	173	228	224	28.0	35.5	38.0
1879	6,901	14,498	14,746	9.2	18.5	20.6	141	295	300	22.8	45.9	50.8
1889	10,064	22,265	22,364	13.4	28.5	31.2	163	360	362	26.4	56.0	61.4
1899	14,746	34,615	32,770	19.6	44.3	45.7	197	463	438	31.9	72.0	74.2
1900	15,507	35,084	33,565	20.7	44.9	46.8	204	461	441	33.0	71.7	74.7
1901	16,493	36,408	34,795	22.0	46.6	48.5	212	468	448	34.3	72.8	75.9
1902	17,646	38,030	35,939	23.5	48.6	50.1	222	479	453	35.9	74.5	76.8
1903	18,687	38,451	37,151	24.9	49.2	51.8	231	475	459	37.4	73.9	77.8
1904	19,087	39,682	37,946	25.4	50.7	52.9	231	480	459	37.4	74.7	77.8
1905	20,421	42,455	39,652	27.2	54.3	55.3	242	504	471	39.2	78.4	79.8
1906	22,087	44,441	41,517	29.4	56.8	57.9	257	518	484	41.6	80.6	82.0
1907	23,251	44,288	42,741	31.0	56.6	59.6	266	506	489	43.0	78.7	82.9
1908	22,276	44,286	41,872	29.7	56.6	58.4	250	497	470	40.5	77.3	79.7
1909	25,319	50,336	46,035	33.7	64.4	64.2	279	555	508	45.1	86.3	86.1

10

Year												
1910	26,942	50,738	47,517	35.9	64.9	66.3	292	550	515	47.2	85.5	87.3
1911	26,831	50,529	47,827	35.7	64.6	66.7	286	539	511	46.3	83.8	86.6
1912	28,088	49,801	48,014	37.4	63.7	67.0	295	524	505	47.7	81.5	85.6
1913	30,018	54,282	51,313	40.0	69.4	71.6	311	562	532	50.3	87.4	90.2
1914	29,701	52,661	50,771	39.6	67.3	70.8	303	538	518	49.0	83.7	87.8
1915	30,957	54,406	51,424	41.2	69.6	71.7	312	548	537	50.5	85.2	87.8
1916	36,980	60,326	54,064	49.3	77.1	75.4	367	599	537	59.4	93.2	91.0
1917	44,583	63,059	54,838	59.4	80.6	76.5	436	617	577	70.6	96.0	91.0
1918	54,868	64,475	59,769	73.1	82.5	83.4	530	622	577	85.8	96.7	97.8
1919	60,599	62,667	59,880	80.7	80.1	83.5	577	597	570	93.4	92.8	96.6
1920	65,583	57,884	58,089	87.4	74.0	81.0	616	543	545	99.7	84.4	92.4
1921	53,582	54,620	56,225	71.4	69.8	78.4	495	505	520	80.1	78.5	88.1
1922	53,912	57,722	58,346	71.8	73.8	81.4	491	525	531	79.4	81.6	90.0
1923	62,304	64,968	64,564	83.0	83.1	90.0	559	582	579	90.5	90.5	98.1
1924	63,336	65,228	65,228	84.4	83.4	91.0	559	576	576	90.5	89.6	97.6
1925	66,363	66,764	66,764	88.4	85.4	93.1	578	581	581	93.8	90.4	98.5
1926	69,663	69,663	69,663	92.8	89.1	97.2	598	598	598	96.8	93.0	101.4
1927	69,961	71,535	69,961	93.2	91.5	97.6	592	605	592	95.8	94.1	100.3
1928	71,684	74,284	69,664	95.5	95.0	97.2	598	620	581	96.8	96.4	98.5
1929	75,069	78,197	71,699	100.0	100.0	100.0	618	643	590	100.0	100.0	100.0
1930	68,363	73,746	69,616	91.1	94.3	97.1	555	599	566	89.8	93.2	95.9
1931	56,504	67,589	64,429	75.3	86.4	89.9	455	545	519	73.6	84.8	88.0
1932	43,497	58,929	56,343	57.9	74.5	78.6	348	466	451	56.3	72.5	76.4
1933	41,137	57,294	54,558	54.8	73.3	76.1	327	456	434	52.9	70.9	73.6
1934	46,559	61,181	58,126	62.0	78.2	81.1	368	483	459	59.5	75.1	77.8
1935	50,781	64,117	59,883	67.6	82.0	83.5	398	503	470	64.4	78.2	79.7
1936	57,039	70,159	63,306	76.0	89.7	88.3	444	546	493	71.8	84.9	83.6
1937	62,952	74,148	66,828	83.9	94.8	93.2	487	574	517	78.8	89.3	87.6
1938³	55,289	66,774	61,364	73.7	85.4	85.6	425	513	472	68.8	79.8	80.0

¹ Cost of Living Index, Federal Reserve Bank of New York and National Industrial Conference Board.
² Price Index, Snyder Index, Federal Reserve Bank of New York and National Industrial Conference Board.
³ Preliminary estimate.

by a collapse in real estate values. Money was tight, and bank failures were numerous.

The year 1829 was marked by economic depression and revival, and the national income per capita in current dollars showed a considerable decline. Yet, on the adjusted basis, there was very little change from the year 1819.

At the end of the next decade, in 1839, national income per capita had recovered somewhat, and on an adjusted basis had risen to approximately the level attained in 1809. The year 1839 was marked by a revival from depression, which was terminated by a financial panic and back failures in October. Harvests were excellent, but prices were falling rapidly.

At the end of the first half of the nineteenth century, in 1849, the peak of the prosperity phase of a business cycle had been reached. Industrial activity was pronounced, widespread railroad construction was proceeding apace, and a California gold rush was beginning. Crops were good, money was easy, and prices were high. Total realized income was $2.4 billion, having increased 48% since 1839. A real advance in per capita income in terms of constant dollars, amounting to some 15% or 20%, had been achieved over the previous decade.

Long-Term Trends, 1849–1899

With the exception of the decade from 1859 to 1869, in which the Civil War took place, the latter half of the nineteenth century witnessed the first part of the amazingly rapid economic growth and industrial development of the United States. Immigrants poured into the country, first from Northern Europe to settle the open country and develop agricultural resources, and then from Southern Europe to settle in cities and provide industrial labor. Railroads were built, and the conquest of a new empire rich in economic resources pushed forward, while cities sprang up as rapid industrialization and urbanization proceeded.

During this half-century the total national income increased over six-fold, from under $2.5 billion to over $15 billion in terms of dollars of constant purchasing power. Per capita income also showed a remarkable advance, rising in constant dollars from under $250 to about $475, or nearly doubling from 1849 to 1899.

The Census Years from 1849 to 1899

The pace of economic progress in the United States increased from the middle of the nineteenth century to the end of the next decade. The year 1859 occurred in the revival part of the business cycle, with business generally active, money easy, commodity prices steady, good crops and satisfactory foreign trade. Total realized income in current dollars increased 78% over 1849, and on an adjusted basis nearly doubled. The population increased 36% in this period, and per capita income on the adjusted basis showed an increase of about 25%.

The Civil War disrupted economic activity, and although inflation brought about an increase of over 50% in income in terms of current dollars from 1859 to 1869, there was actually a decrease in the total in terms of constant dollars. The per capita adjusted income declined about one-fifth. The year 1869 was characterized by relative prosperity in a time of monetary difficulty. In this year crops were good, business was active and railroad building was expanding. The first transcontinental railroad opened for traffic in May. Money, however, was tight, and the cornering of gold on the New York Exchange led up to the Black Friday panic in September.

Total realized income increased only moderately in current dollars from 1869 to 1879, but the rapid decline from the high peak of post-Civil War prices made this slight increase exceedingly effective in terms of dollars of constant purchasing power. Total real income nearly doubled between 1869 and 1879. While per capita realized income showed a decline in

TABLE 3: REALIZED PRIVATE PRODUCTION INCOME, TOTAL AND PER CAPITA, IN CURRENT DOLLARS AND CONSTANT DOLLARS OF 1926 PURCHASING POWER, 1799–1938

Year	Total Realized Private Production Income						Per Capita Realized Private Production Income					
	Millions of Dollars			Indexes, 1929 = 100			Dollars			Indexes, 1929 = 100		
	Current Income	Income Adjusted by the Cost of Living[1]	Income Adjusted by the General Price Level[2]	Current Income	Income Adjusted by the Cost of Living[1]	Income Adjusted by the General Price Level[2]	Current Income	Income Adjusted by the Cost of Living[1]	Income Adjusted by the General Price Level[2]	Current Income	Income Adjusted by the Cost of Living[1]	Income Adjusted by the General Price Level[2]
1799	668	1,100	1,077	1.0	1.5	1.6	129	213	208	22.8	36.1	38.4
1809	901	1,419	1,401	1.3	2.0	2.1	128	201	199	22.6	34.1	36.8
1819	855	1,586	1,538	1.2	2.2	2.3	91	169	164	16.0	28.6	30.3
1829	947	1,998	2,024	1.4	2.8	3.1	75	159	161	13.2	26.9	29.8
1839	1,577	3,186	3,173	2.3	4.4	4.8	95	191	191	16.8	32.4	35.3
1849	2,326	5,112	5,239	3.4	7.1	8.0	103	226	231	18.2	38.3	42.7
1859	4,098	8,646	8,756	6.0	12.1	13.3	134	282	285	23.6	47.8	52.7
1869	6,288	8,285	8,145	9.1	11.5	12.4	166	219	215	29.3	37.1	39.7
1879	6,617	13,901	14,139	9.6	19.4	21.5	135	283	288	23.8	48.0	53.2
1889	9,578	21,190	21,284	13.9	29.5	32.4	155	343	345	27.3	58.1	63.8
1899	13,836	32,479	30,747	20.1	45.3	46.7	185	434	411	32.6	73.6	76.0
1900	14,550	32,919	31,494	21.1	45.9	47.9	191	432	414	33.7	73.2	76.5
1901	15,537	34,298	32,778	22.6	47.8	49.8	200	441	422	35.3	74.7	78.0
1902	16,705	36,002	34,022	24.3	50.2	51.7	210	454	429	37.0	76.9	79.3
1903	17,691	36,401	35,171	25.7	50.7	53.5	218	449	434	38.4	76.1	80.2
1904	18,059	37,545	35,903	26.2	52.3	54.6	219	455	435	38.6	77.1	80.4
1905	19,363	40,256	37,598	28.1	56.1	57.2	230	478	446	40.6	81.0	82.4
1906	21,008	42,270	39,489	30.5	58.9	60.0	245	492	460	43.2	83.4	85.0
1907	22,112	42,118	40,647	32.1	58.7	61.8	253	482	465	44.6	81.7	86.0
1908	21,049	41,847	39,566	30.6	58.3	60.1	236	470	444	41.6	79.7	82.1
1909	24,033	47,779	43,696	34.9	66.6	66.4	265	527	482	46.7	89.3	89.1

14

Year												
1910	25,569	48,153	45,095	37.1	67.1	68.6	277	522	489	48.9	88.5	90.4
1911	25,385	47,806	45,250	36.9	66.6	68.8	271	510	483	47.8	86.4	89.3
1912	26,559	47,090	45,400	38.6	65.6	69.0	279	495	477	49.2	83.9	88.2
1913	28,391	51,340	48,532	41.2	71.6	73.8	294	532	503	51.9	90.2	93.0
1914	27,954	49,564	47,785	40.6	69.1	72.6	285	506	488	50.3	85.8	90.2
1915	29,114	51,167	48,362	42.3	71.3	73.5	293	515	487	51.7	87.3	90.0
1916	35,032	57,148	51,216	50.9	79.7	77.9	348	567	508	61.4	96.1	93.9
1917	42,014	59,426	51,678	61.0	82.8	78.6	411	582	506	72.5	98.6	93.5
1918	49,520	58,190	53,943	71.9	81.1	82.0	478	562	521	84.3	95.3	96.3
1919	55,539	57,434	54,880	80.6	80.1	83.4	529	547	523	93.3	92.7	96.7
1920	60,995	53,835	54,026	88.6	75.0	82.1	572	505	507	100.9	85.6	93.7
1921	48,763	49,707	51,168	70.8	69.3	77.8	451	459	473	79.5	77.8	87.4
1922	49,036	52,501	53,069	71.2	73.2	80.7	446	478	483	78.7	81.0	89.3
1923	57,213	59,659	59,288	83.1	83.2	90.1	513	535	532	90.5	90.7	98.3
1924	58,178	59,916	59,916	84.5	83.5	91.1	514	529	529	90.7	89.7	97.8
1925	60,949	61,317	61,317	88.5	85.5	93.2	531	534	534	93.7	90.5	98.7
1926	63,857	63,857	63,857	92.7	89.0	97.1	548	548	548	96.6	92.9	101.3
1927	63,942	65,380	63,942	92.8	91.1	97.2	541	553	541	95.4	93.7	100.0
1928	65,653	68,034	63,803	95.3	94.8	97.0	548	568	532	96.6	96.3	98.3
1929	68,872	71,742	65,780	100.0	100.0	100.0	567	590	541	100.0	100.0	100.0
1930	61,968	66,848	63,104	90.0	93.2	95.9	503	543	513	88.7	92.0	94.8
1931	50,056	59,888	57,088	72.7	83.5	86.8	403	483	460	71.1	81.9	85.0
1932	37,132	49,708	48,098	53.9	69.3	73.1	297	398	385	52.4	67.5	71.2
1933	35,074	48,850	46,517	50.9	68.1	70.7	279	388	370	49.2	65.8	68.4
1934	40,205	52,832	50,194	58.4	73.6	76.3	318	417	396	56.1	70.7	73.2
1935	44,037	55,602	51,930	63.9	77.5	78.9	345	436	407	60.8	73.9	75.2
1936	49,852	61,319	55,830	72.4	85.5	84.1	388	477	431	68.4	80.8	79.7
1937	54,959	64,734	58,343	79.8	90.2	88.7	425	501	451	75.0	84.9	83.4
1938³	47,468	57,929	52,684	68.9	79.9	80.1	365	441	405	64.4	74.7	74.9

¹ Cost of Living Index, Federal Reserve Bank of New York and National Industrial Conference Board.

² Price Index, Snyder Index, Federal Reserve Bank of New York and National Industrial Conference Board.

³ Preliminary estimate.

this period in terms of current dollars, on the adjusted basis there was an increase of 33%, a greater gain than in any other ten-year period in the nineteenth century.

This decade ushered in a period of exceedingly rapid economic expansion in the United States, both in terms of the actual increase in total income and in per capita income. Between 1869 and the end of the century, total realized income doubled in terms of current dollars and quadrupled in terms of constant purchasing power dollars. Per capita income, on the adjusted basis, just about doubled. The status of each census year from 1879–1899 in relation to the business cycle was as follows:

The year 1879 marked the completion of a revival from depression and the beginning of a period of prosperity; railroad construction was active; farm trade was increasing; money was easy, and specie payments were resumed early in the year; exceptionally large crops were harvested, and high prices were the rule.

The year 1889 was prosperous. There was an enormous volume of business activity, and many records were made in the field of industrial production; financial conditions were relatively easy, with high stock and bond prices; crops were good, though commodity prices were only fair.

The year 1899 was also on the whole prosperous, with rising wages and commodity prices. Extensive promotion of securities led to wild speculation in stocks and a collapse and brief panic on the New York Stock Exchange in December. Large crops were harvested and good prices received, while a boom in immigration was beginning.

ANNUAL ESTIMATES, 1899–1938

The most striking aspect of the total realized national income from 1899 to 1938 is the tremendous increase shown in this short period of time: a rise from $15 billion to $62 billion, or more than quadruple in less than 40 years. This increase, however, was accompanied by a great rise in population over the whole period and a decline in the purchasing power of money following inflation during the World War. When these factors are taken into account, the increase appears to have been of much more modest proportions. The per capita income, adjusted for general price level changes, rose in this period only from $456 to $531.

In using the estimates from the turn of the century to the present time, several outstanding developments of historical importance should be borne in mind. Following a period of comparative prosperity, a financial panic developed at the end of 1907. This interruption was short-lived, however, and from 1910 until the outbreak of the World War conditions of moderate prosperity prevailed. The World War brought about significant shifts in the national income, which will be discussed in subsequent chapters, and brought on an inflation which doubled the total national income in terms of current dollars with very little improvement in the per capita income as adjusted for price level changes. After a short but sharp postwar partial deflation, an era of prosperity reigned until the fall of 1929. Following a three-year descent into deep depression, an irregular improvement was experienced through 1937. The business recession which began early in the fall of 1937 abruptly interrupted recovery, preliminary estimates placing the 1938 national income total over 10% lower than in 1937.

In terms of per capita income adjusted for changes in the cost of living and in price levels, income in 1937 was but little larger than in 1913, though about a fourth higher than in 1899. As has previously been noted in this chapter, some of the economic advance during this period was attained through the shortening of working hours, lightening the most burdensome types of work and improvement in the quality of products.

OTHER INCOME TOTALS

In the foregoing the trends of income have been considered in terms of the estimates of total realized income. Two other classifications of income data that throw further light on certain aspects of economic changes in this period have been compiled and are presented in the rest of this chapter.

Realized Production Income

The realized production income total includes salaries and wages, entrepreneurial income, dividends, interest and net rents and royalties received both from private enterprises and from government. It excludes the miscellaneous items from both private and government sources which are enumerated in Chapters IV and V. The estimates of this total in current dollars and in dollars of constant purchasing power, both total and per capita, are presented in Table 2.

Realized Private Production Income

The realized private production income total includes the same items as the production income total above mentioned, but covers only the private industries and occupations and excludes income of these types derived from government sources. This is a very important total, in that it relates strictly to income derived from private enterprise and excludes all income from government sources and the miscellaneous income items described in Chapter V. This is the proper total to use in considering the industrial origin and the relative importance of the various types of incomes derived from private enterprise activity.

Income from private production sources reached a total of just under $69 billion in 1929 and, after declining 36% by 1935, recovered to just under $55 billion in 1937. A sharp recession reduced this total to about $47.5 billion in 1938.

The most significant figures in Table 3 relate to the per

capita income adjusted for price level changes. This gives a rough measure of the entire volume of goods and services, or real income, per capita which was produced by private enterprise in the years under consideration. There was apparently some decline during the first third of the nineteenth century. As has been previously mentioned, this was a period of considerable national disturbance. The next third of the nineteenth century was a period of dynamic expansion, during which the adjusted per capita income increased by three-fourths. After the setback caused by the Civil War, real per capita income had recovered in 1879 only to about the level of 1859. Again followed a period of rapid expansion, and within the next three decades the per capita income in terms of dollars of constant purchasing power rose by about 75%.

Another setback was caused by the World War. The subsequent improvement up to 1929 has been obliterated in the current depressions, and by 1938 the per capita real income total derived from private production sources was lower than during the years just preceding the World War. This does not mean that there has been no economic progress per capita during these years, for hours of work have been reduced, and the quality of products sold for the same or lower price has advanced. This has been previously mentioned in this chapter. It does indicate, however, that in actual per capita volume of goods and services derived from private enterprise sources there has been little, if any, advance in recent years over the levels which had been reached in the decade prior to the World War. It is apparent from these income data that the period of disturbance ushered in by the War has not yet run its course in the United States.

These movements in the realized private production income of the country were accompanied by—and contrasted with—important changes in the amount and proportion of income derived from government sources. (See Chapter IV.)

CHAPTER II

KINDS OF PRIVATE PRODUCTION INCOME

REASONABLY adequate data by which to estimate the amount of each kind of private production income are available only since the turn of the twentieth century. The distribution of the national income by its sources in the various industries, in the early years and up through the nineteenth century, however, gives some clue as to the probable distribution of income by kind in the earlier period.[1]

The fact of the predominance of agriculture and transportation, combined with our knowledge of the types of enterprises—plantations in the South and individually-operated farms in the North, individually-owned fishing and shipping vessels and small trading enterprises—suggests that income was received primarily in the form of entrepreneurial profits and wages, with practically no dividends and only small receipts of interest, net rents and royalties. In 1899 entrepreneurial income was just under 30% of the total, while salaries and wages accounted for about 58%.

With the continued industrialization and incorporation of enterprises after 1900, a further and striking shift occurred in the kinds of income. While entrepreneurial profits of individual enterprisers declined, as more and more enterprisers became stockholders and salaried employees in incorporated businesses, the ratio of entrepreneurial income to the total decreased. From 1899 to 1937 the proportion dropped from 29% to just over 20%. Meanwhile the importance of salaries and wages in total income increased in this period from 58% to 68%. There was a shift in industrial financing from fixed interest bonds to equity stocks, as well as the transfer of individual enterprisers to the position of stockholders. Partly reflecting these changes, dividends, which have fluctuated

---

[1] See also Willford I. King, "The Wealth and Income of the People of the United States," New York, 1919, Table xxxi, p. 160.

considerably with the state of general business conditions, increased from 6% of the total in 1899 to over 8% in 1937, while the interest proportion tended to decline.

TABLE 4: KINDS OF REALIZED PRIVATE PRODUCTION INCOME, 1899–1937

Millions of Dollars

Year	Salaries and Wages	Entrepreneurial Income	Dividends[1]	Interest[1]	Net Rents and Royalties	Total, All Types
1899	7,968	4,027	834	620	387	13,836
1900	8,475	4,100	938	631	406	14,550
1901	9,148	4,273	1,034	664	418	15,537
1902	9,955	4,463	1,147	699	441	16,705
1903	10,729	4,602	1,153	737	470	17,691
1904	10,912	4,800	1,089	774	484	18,059
1905	12,009	4,863	1,175	813	503	19,363
1906	13,022	5,159	1,432	860	535	21,008
1907	13,607	5,415	1,591	921	578	22,112
1908	12,285	5,706	1,485	982	591	21,049
1909	14,165	6,630	1,567	1,015	656	24,033
1910	15,119	6,887	1,828	1,048	687	25,569
1911	15,281	6,433	1,866	1,094	711	25,385
1912	15,983	6,794	1,950	1,141	691	26,559
1913	17,345	6,942	2,167	1,194	743	28,391
1914	16,975	6,971	2,028	1,211	769	27,954
1915	17,619	7,358	2,055	1,294	788	29,114
1916	20,845	8,654	3,317	1,349	867	35,032
1917	24,629	11,219	3,747	1,425	994	42,014
1918	29,903	13,476	3,520	1,507	1,114	49,520
1919	34,565	14,878	3,209	1,625	1,262	55,539
1920	41,456	13,266	3,090	1,808	1,375	60,995
1921	32,171	10,535	2,937	1,915	1,205	48,763
1922	33,201	10,129	2,634	1,919	1,153	49,036
1923	39,557	11,135	3,299	2,020	1,202	57,213
1924	39,204	12,147	3,424	2,168	1,235	58,178
1925	40,581	12,823	4,014	2,248	1,283	60,949
1926	43,236	12,573	4,439	2,311	1,298	63,857
1927	42,901	12,531	4,765	2,414	1,331	63,942
1928	43,712	12,886	5,157	2,535	1,363	65,653
1929	45,922	13,118	5,763	2,633	1,436	68,872
1930	41,342	11,277	5,631	2,766	952	61,968
1931	33,716	8,955	4,179	2,668	548	50,066
1932	24,964	6,712	2,626	2,409	421	37,132
1933	23,339	7,018	2,102	2,117	498	35,074
1934	27,019	8,123	2,509	1,914	640	40,205
1935	29,539	19,249	2,803	1,702	744	44,037
1936	33,164	10,582	3,831	1,439	836	49,852
1937	37,383	11,128	4,309	1,230	909	54,959

[1] Not adjusted for balance of international payments of dividends and interest.

TABLE 5: PERCENTAGE DISTRIBUTION OF REALIZED PRIVATE PRODUCTION INCOME BY KIND, 1899–1937

Year	Salaries and Wages	Entrepreneurial Income	Dividends	Interest	Net Rents and Royalties
1899	57.6	29.1	6.0	4.5	2.8
1900	58.2	28.2	6.4	4.3	2.8
1901	58.9	27.5	6.7	4.3	2.7
1902	59.6	26.7	6 9	4.2	2.6
1903	60.6	26.0	6.5	4.2	2.7
1904	60.4	26.6	6.0	4.3	2.7
1905	62.0	25.1	6.1	4.2	2.6
1906	62.0	24.6	6.8	4.1	2.5
1907	61.5	24.5	7.2	4.2	2.6
1908	58.4	27.1	7.1	4.7	2.8
1909	58.9	27.6	6.5	4.2	2.7
1910	59.1	26.9	7.1	4.1	2.7
1911	60.2	25.3	7.4	4.3	2.8
1912	60.2	25.6	7.3	4.3	2.6
1913	61.1	24.5	7.6	4.2	2.6
1914	60.7	24.9	7.3	4.3	2.8
1915	60.5	25.3	7.1	4.4	2.7
1916	59.5	24.7	9.5	3.9	2.5
1917	58.6	26.7	8.9	3.4	2.4
1918	60.4	27.2	7.1	3.0	2.2
1919	62.2	26.8	5.8	2.9	2.3
1920	68.0	21.7	5.1	3.0	2.3
1921	66.0	21.6	6.0	3.9	2.5
1922	67.7	20.7	5.4	3.9	2.4
1923	69.1	19.5	5.8	3.5	2.1
1924	67.4	20.9	5.9	3.7	2.1
1925	66.6	21.0	6.6	3.7	2.1
1926	67.7	19.7	7.0	3.6	2.0
1927	67.1	19.6	7.5	3.8	2.1
1928	66.6	19.6	7.9	3.9	2.1
1929	66.7	19.0	8.4	3.8	2.1
1930	66.7	18.2	9.1	4.5	1.5
1931	67.3	17.9	8.3	5.3	1.1
1932	67.2	18.1	7.1	6.5	1.1
1933	66.5	20.0	6.0	6.0	1.4
1934	67.2	20.2	6.2	4.8	1.6
1935	67.1	21.0	6.4	3.9	1.7
1936	66.5	21.2	7.7	2.9	1.7
1937	68.0	20.2	7.8	2.2	1.7

TABLE 6: INDEXES OF REALIZED PRIVATE PRODUCTION INCOME BY KIND, 1899–1937

1929 = 100

Year	Salaries and Wages	Entrepreneurial Income	Dividends	Interest	Net Rents and Royalties	Total, All Types
1899	17.4	30.7	14.5	23.5	26.9	20.1
1900	18.5	31.3	16.3	24.0	28.3	21.1
1901	19.9	32.6	17.9	25.2	29.1	22.6
1902	21.7	34.0	19.9	26.5	30.7	24.3
1903	23.4	35.1	20.0	28.0	32.7	25.7
1904	23.8	36.6	18.9	29.4	33.7	26.2
1905	26.2	37.1	20.4	30.9	35.0	28.1
1906	28.4	39.3	24.8	32.7	37.2	30.5
1907	29.6	41.3	27.6	35.0	40.3	32.1
1908	26.8	43.5	25.8	37.3	42.1	30.6
1909	30.8	50.5	27.2	38.5	45.7	34.9
1910	32.9	52.5	31.7	39.8	47.7	37.1
1911	33.3	49.0	32.4	41.5	49.5	36.9
1912	34.8	51.8	33.8	43.3	48.1	38.6
1913	37.8	52.9	37.6	45.3	51.7	41.2
1914	37.0	53.1	35.2	46.0	53.6	40.6
1915	38.4	56.1	35.7	49.1	54.9	42.3
1916	45.4	66.0	57.6	51.2	60.4	50.9
1917	53.6	85.5	65.0	54.1	69.2	61.0
1918	65.1	102.7	61.1	57.2	77.6	71.9
1919	75.3	113.4	55.7	61.7	87.9	80.6
1920	90.3	101.1	53.6	68.7	95.8	88.6
1921	70.1	80.3	51.0	72.7	83.9	70.8
1922	72.3	77.2	45.7	72.9	80.3	71.2
1923	86.1	84.9	57.2	76.7	83.7	83.1
1924	85.4	92.6	59.4	82.3	86.0	84.5
1925	88.4	97.8	69.7	85.4	89.3	88.5
1926	94.2	95.8	77.0	87.8	90.4	92.7
1927	93.4	95.5	82.7	91.7	92.7	92.8
1928	95.2	98.2	89.5	96.3	94.9	95.3
1929	100.0	100.0	100.0	100.0	100.0	100.0
1930	90.0	86.0	97.7	105.1	66.3	90.0
1931	73.4	68.3	72.5	101.3	38.2	72.7
1932	54.4	51.2	45.6	91.5	29.3	53.9
1933	50.8	53.5	36.5	80.4	34.7	50.9
1934	58.8	61.9	43.5	72.7	44.6	58.4
1935	64.3	70.5	48.6	64.6	51.8	63.9
1936	72.2	80.7	66.5	54.7	58.2	72.4
1937	81.4	84.8	74.8	46.7	63.3	79.8

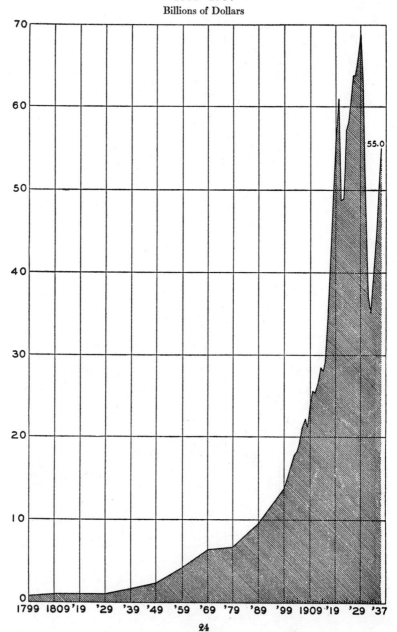

CHART 4: REALIZED PRIVATE PRODUCTION INCOME, 1799–1937

Billions of Dollars

CHART 5: REALIZED PRIVATE PRODUCTION INCOME, BY KIND, 1899–1937

Billions of Dollars

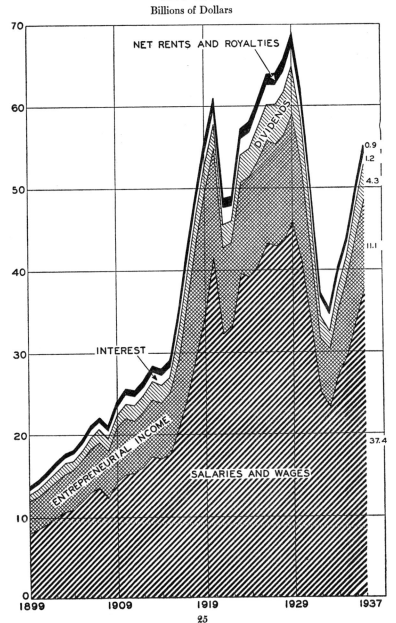

NET RENTS AND ROYALTIES

DIVIDENDS

INTEREST

ENTREPRENEURIAL INCOME

SALARIES AND WAGES

0.9
1.2
4.3
11.1
37.4

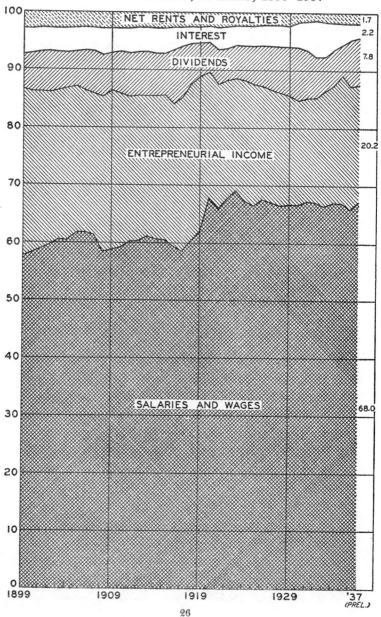

CHART 6: PERCENTAGE DISTRIBUTION OF REALIZED PRIVATE PRODUCTION INCOME, BY KIND, 1899–1937

The most striking change in importance of the various kinds of income in recent years concerns interest. It accounted for just under 4% of the total realized private production income in the years just prior to 1930. Since interest is by nature based on a rate agreed upon to hold for a period of years, it is a stable kind of income. It therefore rose in importance during the subsequent depression when other kinds were falling off, so that in 1932 it accounted for over 6% of the total. Since then it has rapidly declined to an importance of only 2.2% of the total in 1937.

Kinds of Income by Industries

As will be pointed out in the discussion later of distribution of income by industrial origin, the importance of salaries and wages and of other kinds of income varies widely in the different industries because of differences in the kinds of organization most prevalent. In agriculture, in which small, unincorporated enterprises have predominated, dividends are negligible, salaries and wages are a minor item, and entrepreneurial income is the principal kind of return to those engaging, or investing, in the industry. In manufacturing, which in recent years has been carried on mainly by large-scale incorporated enterprises, salaries and wages and dividends account for practically the entire income.

Salaries and Wages

The distribution of salary and wage income by industrial origin is presented in Table 7. The manufacturing, trade and service industries account for nearly two-thirds of the total disbursement of this kind of income by private industries.

In most industries the proportion of income attributable to salaries and wages has remained fairly constant since 1900. In transportation and trade, however, as is indicated in Table 8, the ratio has been steadily increasing, as small independent

TABLE 7: SALARIES AND WAGES, BY INDUSTRIAL ORIGIN, 1899–1937

Millions of Dollars

Year	Agriculture	Mining and Quarrying	Electric Light and Power and Gas	Manufacturing	Construction	Transportation	Communication	Trade	Finance	Service	Miscellaneous	Total, Private Industries
1899	459	289	35	2,181	531	967	39	1,638	202	1,160	467	7,968
1900	526	344	41	2,321	508	1,033	46	1,741	239	1,179	497	8,475
1901	524	405	47	2,548	616	1,095	53	1,848	290	1,186	536	9,148
1902	590	371	46	2,871	682	1,163	59	2,034	347	1,208	584	9,955
1903	615	545	52	3,053	692	1,257	62	2,161	393	1,240	629	10,729
1904	717	509	56	2,891	748	1,331	66	2,252	438	1,264	640	10,912
1905	716	561	56	3,362	858	1,402	82	2,527	454	1,287	704	12,009
1906	827	592	66	3,633	964	1,543	96	2,802	428	1,308	763	13,022
1907	823	754	74	3,928	892	1,614	94	2,873	389	1,368	798	13,607
1908	867	565	76	3,286	721	1,559	92	2,587	412	1,400	720	12,285
1909	855	643	86	3,988	941	1,616	100	2,956	462	1,688	830	14,165
1910	853	709	96	4,507	926	1,753	111	3,088	497	1,693	886	15,119
1911	896	725	104	4,482	901	1,824	127	3,126	539	1,661	896	15,281
1912	900	784	116	4,964	999	1,948	139	3,050	582	1,564	937	15,983
1913	925	867	126	5,310	1,071	2,039	153	3,446	622	1,769	1,017	17,345
1914	901	752	135	4,964	800	2,016	155	3,767	630	1,860	995	16,975
1915	921	758	142	5,310	798	2,078	151	3,893	675	1,860	1,033	17,619
1916	987	953	160	7,051	882	2,372	181	4,283	764	1,990	1,222	20,845
1917	1,229	1,195	176	8,866	856	2,834	214	4,780	840	2,195	1,444	24,629
1918	1,447	1,489	190	11,076	916	3,961	249	5,352	963	2,507	1,753	29,903
1919	1,778	1,532	232	12,348	1,325	4,531	309	6,289	1,267	2,928	2,026	34,565

Year												
1920	2,042	2,192	275	14,563	1,887	5,821	407	6,757	1,507	3,575	2,430	41,456
1921	1,307	1,582	282	9,793	1,382	4,625	405	5,781	1,558	3,570	1,886	32,171
1922	1,272	1,485	300	10,369	1,647	4,430	429	6,224	1,567	3,532	1,946	33,201
1923	1,440	2,111	373	12,894	2,393	4,906	474	7,019	1,740	3,888	2,319	39,557
1924	1,418	1,787	439	12,274	2,407	4,798	508	7,134	1,903	4,238	2,298	39,204
1925	1,473	1,687	457	12,835	2,393	4,859	531	7,536	2,010	4,421	2,379	40,581
1926	1,527	1,963	503	13,411	2,726	5,013	571	7,905	2,192	4,891	2,534	43,236
1927	1,543	1,746	526	13,411	2,634	4,938	590	7,716	2,354	4,928	2,515	42,901
1928	1,554	1,551	565	13,736	2,753	4,857	629	7,831	2,519	5,155	2,562	43,712
1929	1,565	1,614	616	14,770	2,704	4,968	707	8,200	2,696	5,392	2,692	45,922
1930	1,322	1,386	609	12,661	2,371	4,495	715	7,798	2,503	4,977	2,503	41,342
1931	957	978	543	9,901	1,579	3,797	640	6,776	2,215	4,198	2,132	33,716
1932	619	658	440	7,008	728	2,913	534	5,248	1,896	3,233	1,688	24,964
1933	574	658	398	7,045	602	2,719	460	4,625	1,718	2,930	1,608	23,339
1934	615	857	440	8,815	771	2,950	483	5,281	1,807	3,279	1,723	27,019
1935	656	901	467	9,890	861	3,215	504	5,685	1,898	3,619	1,843	29,539
1936	768	1,032	508	11,425	1,185	3,600	605	6,050	1,990	3,910	2,091	33,164
1937	879	1,167	556	13,614	1,482	3,889	702	6,673	2,135	4,229	2,057	37,383

TABLE 8: RATIO OF SALARIES AND WAGES TO TOTAL INCOME, 1899–1937 [1]

Year	Agriculture	Mining and Quarrying	Electric Light and Power and Gas	Manufacturing	Construction	Transportation	Communication	Trade	Service	Miscellaneous	Total, Private Industries
1899	15.6	69.5	60.3	80.4	81.1	65.9	65.0	63.5	66.5	46.1	57.6
1900	17.3	75.9	63.1	78.9	81.0	66.3	68.7	64.0	66.5	46.1	58.2
1901	16.6	73.4	62.7	79.8	81.3	66.6	69.7	64.7	66.4	46.5	58.9
1902	17.7	75.1	59.7	79.6	81.3	67.1	67.8	65.7	66.4	46.9	59.6
1903	17.9	81.2	58.4	80.9	81.2	67.1	65.3	66.0	66.3	47.8	60.6
1904	19.3	78.9	56.6	82.2	81.4	67.2	65.3	66.6	66.4	47.9	60.4
1905	19.5	75.2	54.4	83.4	81.6	67.0	69.5	68.4	66.4	49.0	62.0
1906	20.5	70.9	55.0	83.0	81.5	67.2	70.6	69.7	66.3	48.7	62.0
1907	19.5	71.9	55.2	82.8	81.4	67.2	66.7	68.9	66.3	47.9	61.5
1908	18.8	73.3	54.7	81.2	81.2	65.4	66.2	66.4	66.3	45.5	58.4
1909	16.1	74.9	54.8	82.7	81.6	64.8	64.9	68.6	66.4	47.8	58.9
1910	15.3	74.7	57.1	82.7	81.5	65.2	66.9	68.7	66.2	47.7	59.1
1911	17.1	76.4	54.2	82.1	81.3	66.1	69.0	68.7	66.1	48.9	60.2
1912	15.8	75.5	55.0	82.8	81.6	67.1	68.8	68.9	66.0	50.6	60.2
1913	16.6	73.3	55.3	82.8	81.6	67.1	69.2	67.8	65.7	51.5	61.1
1914	16.3	74.6	54.0	82.6	81.6	66.7	68.3	68.4	65.7	51.9	60.7
1915	15.6	74.6	53.0	83.0	81.8	66.6	66.8	68.6	65.6	52.8	60.5
1916	14.0	65.6	53.5	80.6	81.7	68.4	69.3	68.9	65.5	46.9	59.5
1917	12.8	67.4	53.0	81.8	81.1	71.4	70.9	68.5	65.4	48.7	58.6
1918	12.5	73.7	50.9	84.7	80.9	78.2	72.6	68.2	65.5	53.3	60.4
1919	14.0	80.2	54.1	86.1	81.1	79.7	75.9	68.5	65.6	56.8	62.2

Year											
1920	68.0	63.3	65.8	67.2	79.8	83.6	84.8	86.6	57.3	83.4	19.3
1921	66.0	55.6	65.8	67.9	77.9	80.3	80.3	83.3	56.4	79.8	17.3
1922	67.7	62.5	65.8	70.5	78.1	78.2	78.7	84.3	52.7	80.5	18.1
1923	69.1	65.7	65.6	72.2	77.6	79.2	84.7	84.4	52.2	80.8	18.2
1924	67.4	61.3	65.5	71.5	77.1	78.1	83.8	84.1	51.4	78.5	16.6
1925	66.6	61.7	65.2	72.4	75.3	77.5	79.2	83.3	48.8	75.2	16.3
1926	67.7	59.3	65.1	72.7	75.5	77.9	86.7	82.9	48.6	76.3	17.7
1927	67.1	57.7	64.8	72.1	74.6	76.5	85.1	82.4	47.1	75.2	17.9
1928	66.6	57.3	64.8	72.0	75.7	76.7	84.5	81.2	44.8	73.9	17.7
1929	66.7	57.2	64.4	71.6	76.3	76.1	83.8	81.8	44.3	70.3	17.9
1930	66.7	57.3	63.1	73.4	74.0	74.3	81.5	79.3	39.1	72.3	19.6
1931	67.3	57.9	60.9	74.2	70.9	73.8	81.2	80.0	36.7	73.9	21.4
1932	67.2	57.2	59.8	75.1	68.0	72.4	78.1	82.2	32.9	70.8	20.4
1933	66.5	58.6	59.9	75.4	64.6	72.8	79.0	83.6	34.4	72.9	15.2
1934	67.2	57.5	60.7	77.1	65.8	72.7	83.1	84.2	38.5	73.1	13.2
1935	67.1	57.1	60.2	77.8	66.6	73.9	82.6	84.4	40.3	72.5	11.9
1936	66.5	57.6	58.7	78.5	71.3	75.7	81.9	80.8	41.9	69.7	12.0
1937	68.0	57.0	59.3	79.3	74.4	77.9	82.1	81.9	44.0	67.0	13.0

[1] Finance industry omitted; see text, p. 56.

TABLE 9: INDEXES OF SALARIES AND WAGES, BY INDUSTRIAL ORIGIN, 1899–1937

1929 = 100

Year	Agriculture	Mining and Quarrying	Electric Light and Power and Gas	Manufacturing	Construction	Transportation	Communication	Trade	Finance	Service	Miscellaneous	Total, Private Industries
1899	29.3	17.9	5.7	14.8	19.6	19.5	5.5	20.0	7.5	21.5	17.3	17.4
1900	33.6	21.3	6.7	15.7	18.8	20.8	6.5	21.2	8.9	21.9	18.5	18.5
1901	33.5	25.1	7.6	17.3	22.8	22.0	7.5	22.5	10.8	22.0	19.9	19.9
1902	37.7	23.0	7.5	19.4	25.2	23.4	8.3	24.8	12.9	22.4	21.7	21.7
1903	39.3	33.8	8.4	20.9	25.6	25.3	8.8	26.4	14.6	23.0	23.4	23.4
1904	45.8	31.5	9.1	19.6	27.7	26.8	9.3	27.5	16.2	23.4	23.8	23.8
1905	45.8	34.8	9.1	22.8	31.7	28.2	11.6	30.8	16.8	23.9	26.2	26.2
1906	52.8	36.7	10.7	24.6	35.7	31.1	13.6	34.2	15.9	24.3	28.3	28.4
1907	52.6	46.7	12.0	26.6	33.0	32.5	13.3	35.0	14.4	25.4	29.6	29.6
1908	55.4	35.0	12.3	22.2	26.7	31.4	13.0	31.5	15.3	26.0	26.7	26.8
1909	54.6	39.8	14.0	27.0	34.8	32.5	14.1	36.0	17.1	31.3	30.9	30.8
1910	54.5	43.9	15.6	30.5	34.2	35.3	15.7	37.7	18.4	31.4	32.9	32.9
1911	57.3	44.9	16.9	30.3	33.3	36.7	18.0	38.1	20.0	30.8	33.3	33.3
1912	57.5	48.6	18.8	33.6	36.9	39.2	19.7	37.2	21.6	29.0	34.9	34.8
1913	59.1	53.7	20.5	36.0	39.6	41.0	21.6	42.0	23.1	32.8	37.9	37.8
1914	57.6	46.6	21.9	33.6	29.6	40.6	21.9	45.9	23.4	34.5	37.1	37.0
1915	58.8	47.0	23.1	36.0	29.5	41.8	21.4	47.5	25.0	34.5	38.5	38.4
1916	63.1	59.0	26.0	47.7	32.6	47.7	25.6	52.2	28.3	36.9	45.6	45.4
1917	78.5	74.0	28.6	60.0	31.7	57.0	30.3	58.3	31.2	40.7	53.9	53.6
1918	92.5	92.3	30.8	75.0	33.9	79.7	35.2	65.3	35.7	46.5	65.6	65.1
1919	113.6	94.9	37.7	83.6	49.0	91.2	43.7	76.7	47.0	54.3	75.8	75.3

Year												
1920	130.5	135.8	44.6	98.6	69.8	117.2	57.6	82.4	55.9	66.3	90.9	90.3
1921	83.5	98.0	45.8	66.3	51.1	93.1	57.3	70.5	57.8	66.2	71.0	70.1
1922	81.8	92.0	48.7	70.2	60.9	89.2	60.7	75.9	58.1	65.5	73.3	72.3
1923	92.0	130.8	60.6	87.3	88.5	98.8	67.0	85.6	64.5	72.1	87.1	86.1
1924	90.6	110.7	71.3	83.1	89.0	96.6	71.9	87.0	70.6	78.6	86.2	85.4
1925	94.1	104.5	74.2	86.9	88.5	97.8	75.1	91.9	74.6	82.0	89.3	88.4
1926	97.6	121.6	81.7	90.8	100.8	100.9	80.8	96.4	81.3	90.7	95.0	94.2
1927	98.6	108.2	85.4	90.8	97.4	99.4	83.5	94.1	87.3	91.4	94.0	93.4
1928	99.3	96.1	91.7	93.0	101.8	97.8	89.0	95.5	93.4	95.6	95.8	95.2
1929	100.0	100.0	100.0	100.0	100.0	100.0	100.0	100.0	100.0	100.0	100.0	100.0
1930	84.5	85.9	98.9	85.7	87.7	90.5	101.1	95.1	92.8	92.3	93.0	90.0
1931	61.2	60.6	88.1	67.0	58.4	76.4	90.5	82.6	82.2	77.9	79.2	73.4
1932	39.6	40.8	71.4	47.4	26.9	58.6	75.5	64.0	70.3	60.0	62.7	54.4
1933	36.7	40.8	64.6	47.7	22.3	54.7	65.1	56.4	63.8	54.3	59.7	50.8
1934	39.3	53.1	71.4	59.7	28.5	59.4	68.3	64.4	67.0	60.8	64.0	58.8
1935	41.9	55.8	75.8	67.0	31.8	64.7	71.3	69.3	70.4	67.1	68.5	64.3
1936	49.1	63.9	82.5	77.4	43.8	72.5	85.6	73.8	73.8	72.5	77.7	72.2
1937	56.2	72.3	90.3	92.2	54.8	78.3	99.3	81.4	79.2	78.4	76.4	81.4

enterprises have grown into, or merged with, larger corporate enterprises.

Since the World War, salaries and wages have accounted for about two-thirds of the total income derived from private industries, with remarkably little deviation from year to year. The ratios of salaries and wages vary from industry to industry, of course, according to the importance of the labor contribution to production. In agriculture this kind of income has accounted in most years for less than 20% of the total,[1] whereas in manufacturing and construction it has been over 80%.

Entrepreneurial Income

Income derived from independent and unincorporated businesses by private enterprisers, as shown in Table 10, is of primary importance in three industrial groups. Agriculture, trade and the service industries supply four-fifths of the total entrepreneurial income.

According to the Census of Occupations, there were just over 9 million persons in the self-employed group in 1930, or 18.2% of the gainfully occupied population. About 6 million were farmers and 1.7 million were retail dealers. Aside from these, the largest number of individual enterprisers is found in the ranks of the private professions—doctors, dentists, lawyers, clergymen and private tutors.

Estimates for this kind of income are not nearly so well based as for other kinds, and a word of caution against using them for precise comparisons is in order. The estimates for agriculture are fair,[2] for trade they are reasonable assumptions based upon earnings of trade corporations and average wages in the industry, and for professional practitioners they are extensions of sample survey data.

[1] The return on the labor contributed by the farm operator is, of course, included in entrepreneurial income, and this percentage refers only to hired labor.

[2] See Robert F. Martin, "Income in Agriculture, 1929–1935," National Industrial Conference Board, 1936.

As shown in Table 11, notable declines in the importance of this kind of income have been recorded since the turn of the century in trade, where it is still an important item, and in manufacturing and mining, in which the development of large-scale corporate enterprises had already reduced it to a minor position. As an exception to the general rule, after the World War and in the depressions since 1929, the rise of individual trucking and taxi enterprises has caused entrepreneurial income in transportation to increase in relative importance.

Dividend Income

Dividends originating—that is, dividends paid less dividends received by corporations—in each industrial group within which the bulk of the corporations' activities fall, are presented in Table 13. Manufacturing corporations accounted for about a third of all dividend income prior to the World War, but its proportion has risen to about half in more recent years.

Reflecting the relative unimportance of the corporate form of enterprise in some industries, very low proportions for dividends compared with total income are shown for agriculture, construction, trade and service. (See entrepreneurial income section above for reverse income aspect of this situation.) The relatively larger importance of capital investment in public utilities, such as the electric light and power and gas industries and the communications industry, is reflected in a larger proportion of income yielded in the form of dividends on capital stock.

Interest on Private Long-Term Debt

The industrial sources of interest received by individuals from long-term investments in bonds and mortgages annually since 1899 are shown in Table 14.

Interest is most important, of course, in government (see Chapter IV), which carries on a part of its financing through the issuance of interest-bearing bonds, and in those private industries in which the capital investment is necessarily high in relation to the labor contribution to production. In the case of the light and power and transportation utilities, interest has accounted for about a fifth and between 10% and 20% respectively of the total income derived by individuals from these industries. In agriculture, the predominance of individual ownership by farm operators has led to the inclusion of the major portion of the return on capital investment in the entrepreneurial income received by farm operators. In this case only the interest arising from borrowing on agricultural mortgages appears in the national income, so that the interest shown does not reflect the full importance of fixed capital.

In the private industries, interest on long-term debt is derived largely from agriculture, transportation, and electric light and power, which have accounted for about 70% of the total. (See Table 14.)

Some of the interest attributed to each industry in these estimates does not flow directly to individuals. A portion of this interest may go, for example, to insurance companies which have farm mortgages in their investment portfolios. In this case, the interest on farm mortgages held by insurance companies is shown here as income derived from agriculture, since agriculture is the *source*, although this interest is really *received* by insurance companies, classified under the heading of finance.

It has been found necessary to deduct such amounts received by industries to obtain the total received by individuals; and farm mortgage interest received by insurance companies appears as a negative item, therefore, under the heading of insurance companies. Hence these figures show the importance of each industry as a net *source* of interest on long-term indebtedness, although they do not show amounts *directly* received by individuals from each industry.

Notable developments have taken place in the field of agriculture in recent years, that is, during the depressions subsequent to 1929. Both the outstanding indebtedness and the interest rates have declined, the former primarily through foreclosures, and the latter because of government intervention for the purpose of easing credit and forcing the interest rates down.

In contrast to the situation in agriculture, the trend of interest after 1929 in the electric light and power and gas utilities continued to increase, and interest rates declined only moderately, so that the 1937 total was still above that of 1929. Interest is not a large item in the manufacturing income total and was drastically reduced in the recent depressions, so that in 1937 the volume was less than half of that for 1930.

Before the recent depressions, transportation represented the largest private industrial source of long-term interest and accounted for about a fourth of the total. There has been a decline of 35% since 1929.

A striking change has taken place in interest in the finance classification of income by industrial sources. This is discussed in the finance section of Chapter III.

Net Rents and Royalties

As in the case of interest, more rents and royalties are received in some industrial classifications than are disbursed, and the industrial classification, therefore, indicates simply the source of this type of income. It is only the total that reflects the amount *received by individuals*, since the amounts under each industry indicate merely the net rents and royalties as a whole *derived from* that industry.

Two industries, agriculture and trade, account for over three-fourths of the net rents and royalties in the national income.   In both of these industries net rents account for practically the entire totals.   In mining and quarrying and in some branches of manufacturing, royalties are probably the more important part.

Of particular interest in Table 15 are the negative amounts shown for finance, service and the miscellaneous industries. More net rents and royalties were received than disbursed by the business enterprises in these classifications, and a deduction was necessary to obtain a total for all industries which reflected the aggregate amounts received by individuals.[1]

[1] See page 35 (Interest).

TABLE 10: ENTREPRENEURIAL INCOME, BY INDUSTRIAL ORIGIN, 1899–1937

Millions of Dollars

Year	Agriculture	Mining and Quarrying	Manufacturing	Construction	Transportation	Trade	Service	Miscellaneous	Total, All Industries
1899	2,125	17	172	116	72	612	587	326	4,027
1900	2,150	19	179	111	73	631	596	341	4,100
1901	2,250	20	191	134	73	650	600	355	4,273
1902	2,350	18	211	149	70	679	611	375	4,463
1903	2,400	21	223	151	74	710	627	396	4,602
1904	2,550	20	206	163	81	729	640	411	4,800
1905	2,500	20	238	187	87	752	651	428	4,863
1906	2,700	20	256	210	89	776	662	446	5,159
1907	2,850	21	275	194	86	821	692	476	5,415
1908	3,200	18	229	157	82	828	708	484	5,706
1909	3,831	18	277	205	80	859	854	506	6,630
1910	4,044	20	300	202	79	876	857	509	6,887
1911	3,638	20	291	197	78	870	840	499	6,433
1912	4,073	21	312	218	82	829	791	468	6,794
1913	3,899	23	325	234	86	950	895	530	6,942
1914	3,870	21	296	175	95	1,014	941	559	6,971
1915	4,228	21	296	174	111	1,028	941	559	7,358
1916	5,215	28	356	192	143	1,115	1,007	598	8,654
1917	7,372	35	419	187	186	1,248	1,110	662	11,219
1918	9,046	45	500	200	218	1,442	1,269	756	13,476
1919	9,675	46	539	289	261	1,705	1,481	882	14,878
1920	7,211	59	548	310	271	1,991	1,809	1,067	13,266
1921	4,980	49	428	297	274	1,646	1,806	1,055	10,535
1922	4,562	47	426	409	288	1,573	1,787	1,037	10,129
1923	5,269	52	406	385	318	1,608	1,967	1,130	11,135
1924	5,884	44	404	423	341	1,683	2,144	1,224	12,147
1925	6,284	41	406	556	364	1,666	2,237	1,269	12,823
1926	5,803	40	397	361	382	1,721	2,474	1,395	12,573
1927	5,722	38	384	398	386	1,714	2,493	1,396	12,531
1928	5,843	35	378	438	393	1,737	2,608	1,454	12,886
1929	5,797	32	378	439	410	1,823	2,728	1,510	13,118
1930	4,372	34	323	432	383	1,697	2,639	1,398	11,277
1931	2,720	35	274	309	352	1,543	2,477	1,244	8,955
1932	1,758	34	156	169	316	1,287	2,025	967	6,712
1933	2,485	31	159	130	309	1,122	1,877	905	7,018
1934	3,224	32	184	134	353	1,144	2,044	1,007	8,123
1935	3,958	33	196	160	392	1,154	2,286	1,069	9,240
1936	4,616	36	276	234	441	1,144	2,613	1,222	10,582
1937	4,839	39	329	294	459	1,176	2,761	1,231	11,128

TABLE 11: RATIO OF ENTREPRENEURIAL INCOME TO TOTAL INCOME, 1899–1937

Year	Agricul-ture	Mining and Quarrying	Manufac-turing	Construc-tion	Transpor-tation	Trade	Service	Miscella-neous	Total, Private Industries
1899	72.5	4.1	6.3	17.7	4.9	23.7	33.6	32.2	29.1
1900	70.9	4.2	6.1	17.7	4.7	23.2	33.6	31.7	28.2
1901	71.4	3.6	6.0	17.7	4.4	22.7	33.6	30.8	27.5
1902	70.5	3.6	5.9	17.8	4.0	21.9	33.6	30.1	26.7
1903	69.8	3.1	5.8	17.7	4.0	21.7	33.5	30.1	26.0
1904	68.8	3.1	5.9	17.7	4.1	21.6	33.6	30.8	26.6
1905	68.0	2.7	5.9	17.8	4.2	20.4	33.6	29.8	25.1
1906	67.0	2.4	5.8	17.8	3.9	19.3	33.6	28.5	24.6
1907	67.6	2.0	5.8	17.7	3.4	19.7	33.5	28.6	24.5
1908	69.2	2.3	5.7	17.7	3.4	21.3	33.5	30.6	27.1
1909	72.1	2.1	5.7	17.8	3.2	19.9	33.6	29.2	27.6
1910	72.7	2.1	5.5	17.8	2.9	19.5	33.5	27.4	26.9
1911	69.4	2.1	5.3	17.8	2.8	19.1	33.4	27.2	25.3
1912	71.7	2.0	5.2	17.8	2.8	18.7	33.4	25.3	25.6
1913	70.1	1.9	5.1	17.8	2.8	18.7	33.2	26.8	24.5
1914	70.1	2.1	4.9	17.9	3.1	18.4	33.2	29.2	24.9
1915	71.4	2.1	4.6	17.8	3.6	18.1	33.2	28.6	25.3
1916	73.7	1.9	4.1	17.8	4.1	17.9	33.1	23.0	24.7
1917	76.9	2.0	3.9	17.7	4.7	17.9	33.1	22.3	26.7
1918	78.0	2.2	3.8	17.7	4.3	18.4	33.1	23.0	27.2
1919	76.2	2.4	3.8	17.7	4.6	18.6	33.2	24.7	26.8
1920	68.2	2.2	3.3	13.9	3.9	19.8	33.3	27.8	21.7
1921	65.8	2.5	3.6	17.3	4.8	19.3	33.3	31.1	21.6
1922	64.8	2.5	3.5	19.6	5.1	17.8	33.3	33.3	20.7
1923	66.6	2.0	2.7	13.6	5.1	16.5	33.2	32.0	19.5
1924	69.0	1.9	2.8	14.7	5.6	16.9	33.1	32.6	20.9
1925	69.5	1.8	2.6	18.4	5.8	16.0	33.0	32.9	21.0
1926	67.4	1.6	2.5	11.5	5.9	15.8	33.0	32.6	19.7
1927	66.5	1.6	2.4	12.9	6.0	16.0	32.8	32.0	19.6
1928	66.7	1.7	2.2	13.4	6.2	16.0	32.8	32.5	19.6
1929	66.5	1.4	2.1	13.6	6.3	15.9	32.6	32.1	19.0
1930	64.7	1.8	2.0	14.8	6.3	16.0	33.5	32.0	18.2
1931	60.8	2.6	2.2	15.9	6.8	16.9	36.0	33.8	17.9
1932	57.8	3.7	1.8	18.1	7.9	18.4	37.4	32.8	18.1
1933	65.9	3.4	1.9	17.1	8.3	18.3	38.4	33.0	20.0
1934	69.2	2.7	1.8	14.4	8.7	16.7	37.8	33.6	20.2
1935	71.7	2.7	1.7	15.3	9.0	15.8	38.0	33.1	21.0
1936	72.4	2.4	2.0	16.2	9.3	14.8	39.2	33.6	21.2
1937	71.6	2.2	2.0	16.3	9.2	14.0	38.7	34.1	20.2

40

TABLE 12: INDEXES OF ENTREPRENEURIAL INCOME, BY INDUSTRIAL ORIGIN, 1899–1937

1929 = 100

Year	Agriculture	Mining and Quarrying	Manufacturing	Construction	Transportation	Trade	Service	Miscellaneous	Total, All Industries
1899	36.7	53.1	45.5	26.4	17.6	33.6	21.5	21.6	30.7
1900	37.1	59.4	47.4	25.3	17.8	34.6	21.8	22.6	31.3
1901	38.8	62.5	50.5	30.5	17.8	35.7	22.0	23.5	32.6
1902	40.5	56.3	55.8	33.9	17.1	37.2	22.4	24.8	34.0
1903	41.4	65.6	59.0	34.4	18.0	38.9	23.0	26.2	35.1
1904	44.0	62.5	54.5	37.1	19.8	40.0	23.5	27.2	36.6
1905	43.1	62.5	63.0	42.6	21.2	41.3	23.9	28.3	37.1
1906	46.6	62.5	67.7	47.8	21.7	42.6	24.3	29.5	39.3
1907	49.2	65.6	72.8	44.2	21.0	45.0	25.4	31.5	41.3
1908	55.2	56.3	60.6	35.8	20.0	45.4	26.0	32.1	43.5
1909	66.1	56.3	73.3	46.7	19.5	47.1	31.3	33.5	50.5
1910	69.8	62.5	79.4	46.0	19.3	48.1	31.4	33.7	52.5
1911	62.8	62.5	77.0	44.9	19.0	47.7	30.8	33.0	49.0
1912	70.3	65.6	82.5	49.7	20.0	45.5	29.0	31.0	51.8
1913	67.3	71.9	86.0	53.3	21.0	52.1	32.8	35.1	52.9
1914	66.8	65.6	78.3	39.9	23.2	55.6	34.5	37.0	53.1
1915	72.9	65.6	78.3	39.6	27.1	56.4	34.5	37.0	56.1
1916	90.0	87.5	94.2	43.7	34.9	61.2	36.9	39.6	66.0
1917	127.2	109.4	110.8	42.6	45.4	68.5	40.7	43.8	85.5
1918	156.0	140.6	132.3	45.6	53.2	79.1	46.5	50.1	102.7
1919	166.9	143.8	142.6	65.8	63.7	93.5	54.3	58.4	113.4
1920	124.4	184.4	145.0	70.6	66.1	109.2	66.3	70.7	101.1
1921	85.9	153.1	113.2	67.7	66.8	90.3	66.2	69.9	80.3
1922	78.7	146.9	112.7	93.2	70.2	86.3	65.5	68.7	77.2
1923	90.9	162.5	107.4	87.7	77.6	88.2	72.1	74.8	84.9
1924	101.5	137.5	106.9	96.4	83.2	92.3	78.6	81.1	92.6
1925	108.4	128.1	107.4	126.7	88.8	91.4	82.0	84.0	97.8
1926	100.1	125.0	105.0	82.2	93.2	94.4	90.7	92.4	95.8
1927	98.7	118.8	101.6	90.7	94.1	94.0	91.4	92.5	95.5
1928	100.8	109.4	100.0	99.8	95.9	95.3	95.6	96.3	98.2
1929	100.0	100.0	100.0	100.0	100.0	100.0	100.0	100.0	100.0
1930	75.4	106.3	85.4	98.4	93.4	93.1	96.7	92.6	86.0
1931	46.9	109.4	72.5	70.4	85.9	84.6	90.8	82.4	68.3
1932	30.3	106.3	41.3	38.5	77.1	70.6	74.2	64.0	51.2
1933	42.9	96.9	42.1	29.6	75.4	61.5	68.8	59.9	53.5
1934	55.6	100.0	48.7	30.5	86.1	62.8	74.9	66.7	61.9
1935	68.3	103.1	51.9	30.4	95.6	63.3	83.8	70.7	70.5
1936	79.6	112.5	73.0	53.3	107.6	62.8	95.8	80.9	80.7
1937	83.5	121.9	87.0	67.0	112.0	64.5	101.2	81.5	84.8

41

TABLE 13: DIVIDENDS ORIGINATING IN ALL CORPORATIONS, BY INDUSTRIES, 1899–1937

Millions of Dollars

Year	Agriculture	Mining and Quarrying	Electric Light and Power and Gas	Manufacturing	Construction	Transportation	Communication	Trade	Finance	Service	Miscellaneous	Dividends[1] Received by Government	Total,[2] All Industries
1899	11	79	10	285	6	123	16	55	89	9	151	...	834
1900	8	57	11	357	6	145	16	67	91	11	169	...	938
1901	13	91	12	369	6	156	18	70	100	12	187	...	1,034
1902	9	64	13	433	6	170	21	81	130	13	207	...	1,147
1903	8	59	15	413	7	201	25	82	121	14	208	...	1,153
1904	10	67	17	327	5	211	27	72	144	12	197	...	1,089
1905	15	109	19	333	4	229	27	75	139	13	212	...	1,175
1906	23	163	21	383	6	277	27	88	170	15	259	...	1,432
1907	29	204	24	429	7	293	29	97	176	16	287	...	1,591
1908	18	123	23	419	7	297	26	96	192	16	268	...	1,485
1909	18	127	28	439	4	323	36	102	190	17	283	...	1,567
1910	20	142	30	519	5	368	38	132	210	22	342	...	1,828
1911	17	124	37	563	7	360	39	154	224	26	315	...	1,866
1912	21	148	41	598	4	357	43	164	229	27	318	...	1,950
1913	28	200	44	656	4	379	44	247	229	41	295	...	2,167
1914	20	142	54	628	2	383	45	258	224	43	229	...	2,028
1915	19	135	60	668	—	359	48	280	218	47	221	...	2,055
1916	49	349	67	1,198	2	374	51	307	229	51	640	...	3,317
1917	56	404	74	1,383	9	369	57	375	243	62	715	...	3,747
1918	47	338	83	1,315	12	327	59	385	253	64	637	...	3,520
1919	27	195	90	1,262	15	317	59	401	270	67	506	...	3,209
1920	29	210	89	1,488	22	271	59	382	292	64	184	...	3,090
1921	27	193	90	1,324	33	237	67	320	309	53	284	...	2,937
1922	19	139	120	1,311	31	299	80	302	329	50	−46[3]	...	2,634
1923	20	223	161	1,761	38	303	93	369	363	70	−109[3]	...	3,299
1924	19	213	194	1,651	33	315	106	390	385	73	45	...	3,424

42

Year													Total
1925	22	269	230	1,908	60	365	118	440	487	94	21		4,014
1926	20	327	243	2,117	42	375	129	471	466	108	141		4,439
1927	32	278	273	2,225	49	473	144	495	459	110	227		4,765
1928	33	253	346	2,505	53	430	150	499	568	102	218		5,157
1929	20	365	413	2,575	64	502	168	566	711	120	258		5,763
1930	13	249	565	2,613	88	498	202	497	578	119	209		5,631
1931	17	138	506	1,894	42	342	217	386	492	79	66		4,179
1932	6	82	449	1,116	23	137	192	214	308	56	44	[4]	2,626
1933	4	75	324	1,009	20	117	191	179	165	34	−13[3]		2,102
1934	17	107	272	1,255	14	188	190	202	191	42	31	− 9[3]	2,500
1935	20	118	270	1,421	13	191	193	207	207	80	82	−21[3]	2,782
1936	23	178	305	2,239	18	209	183	248	227	110	91	−20[3]	3,811
1937	25	243	336	2,508	20	225	182	296	248	125	101	−12[3]	4,297

[1] Dividends received by the Reconstruction Finance Corporation on preferred stock of private corporations.

[2] Not adjusted for balance of international payments of dividends.

[3] A minus sign indicates that more dividends are received by an industry than are paid.

[4] Less than $500,000.

Millions of Dollars

TABLE 14: INTEREST ON PRIVATE LONG-TERM DEBT,[1] BY INDUSTRIAL ORIGIN, 1899–1937

Year	Agriculture	Mining and Quarrying	Electric Light and Power and Gas	Manufacturing	Construction	Transportation	Communication	Trade	Finance[2]	Service	Miscellaneous	Total, Private Industries
1899	114	5	13	47	2	306	5	5	47	1	75	620
1900	113	5	13	52	2	308	5	5	51	1	76	631
1901	122	6	16	53	2	320	5	5	53	1	81	664
1902	131	6	18	55	2	330	7	7	56	1	86	699
1903	139	7	22	57	2	341	8	8	62	1	90	737
1904	146	8	26	58	3	357	8	8	64	1	95	774
1905	153	8	28	60	3	374	9	9	66	2	101	813
1906	159	9	33	62	3	386	13	13	72	2	108	860
1907	164	10	36	64	3	410	18	18	80	3	115	921
1908	170	10	39	65	3	447	21	21	81	4	121	982
1909	174	11	42	67	3	474	17	17	80	3	127	1,015
1910	184	12	41	68	3	486	16	16	89	3	130	1,048
1911	194	13	50	69	3	498	17	17	93	5	135	1,094
1912	203	14	53	70	3	516	19	19	99	6	139	1,141
1913	210	15	57	72	3	534	22	22	108	6	145	1,194
1914	221	16	59	73	3	526	25	25	110	8	145	1,211
1915	236	17	64	75	4	571	25	25	113	9	155	1,294
1916	262	19	70	77	4	576	27	27	117	12	158	1,349
1917	302	20	80	79	4	577	28	28	132	14	161	1,425
1918	351	22	98	81	4	564	31	31	145	17	163	1,507
1919	411	25	105	85	4	576	35	35	159	20	170	1,625

1920	466	33	114	107	5	601	40	45	193	26	178	1,808
1921	473	42	126	137	8	625	44	43	199	31	187	1,915
1922	484	36	146	105	4	649	35	42	190	35	193	1,919
1923	483	41	178	117	7	668	39	24	216	46	201	2,020
1924	483	56	218	154	10	685	40	33	227	59	203	2,168
1925	486	59	246	152	13	683	50	33	245	73	208	2,248
1926	485	51	286	151	14	663	50	27	272	88	224	2,311
1927	496	48	313	152	14	653	51	33	290	122	242	2,414
1928	494	46	345	183	12	653	45	46	312	141	258	2,535
1929	473	46	358	210	17	644	44	60	317	196	268	2,633
1930	422	41	379	244	17	667	39	68	397	211	281	2,766
1931	352	43	425	225	14	654	39	64	418	180	253	2,668
1932	294	37	447	192	12	656	53	55	276	125	262	2,409
1933	303	36	431	172	10	586	56	49	150	72	251	2,117
1934	279	34	429	161	10	565	56	43	31	64	243	1,914
1935	269	33	419	149	9	554	55	35	−125	62	242	1,702
1936	277	35	396	132	9	507	55	31	−293	55	235	1,439
1937	273	37	369	108	9	418	54	31	−347	49	229	1,230

¹ Received by individuals.   ² A minus sign indicates that more interest is received by an industry than is paid.

45

TABLE 15: NET RENTS AND ROYALTIES, BY INDUSTRIAL ORIGIN, 1899–1937

Millions of Dollars

Year	Agriculture	Mining and Quarrying	Electric Light and Power and Gas	Manufacturing	Construction	Transportation[1]	Communication	Trade	Finance[1]	Service[1]	Miscellaneous[1]	Total, All Industries
1899	224	26	2	29	:	:	:	268	-142	-12	-6	387
1900	237	28	2	32	:	:	:	276	-148	-13	-6	406
1901	244	30	2	32	:	:	:	285	-153	-13	-7	418
1902	255	35	2	35	:	:	:	297	-161	-13	-7	441
1903	277	39	2	36	:	:	:	311	-172	-13	-8	470
1904	285	41	2	37	:	:	:	319	-177	-13	-8	484
1905	294	48	2	39	:	:	:	329	-185	-14	-8	503
1906	320	51	2	43	:	:	:	340	-196	-14	-9	535
1907	348	60	2	47	:	:	:	359	-212	-15	-9	578
1908	366	55	1	47	:	:	:	362	-216	-15	-9	591
1909	433	60	1	53	2	1	1	376	-240	-18	-11	656
1910	462	66	1	53	2	1	1	384	-252	-18	-11	687
1911	496	67	1	53	2	1	1	381	-260	-18	-11	711
1912	482	72	1	52	2	1	1	363	-253	-17	-11	691
1913	497	78	1	52	2	1	2	416	-273	-19	-12	743
1914	506	77	2	51	2	1	2	444	-282	-20	-12	769
1915	517	85	2	52	2	1	2	451	-289	-20	-13	788
1916	559	103	2	65	2	1	2	488	-318	-21	-14	867
1917	631	119	2	96	2	1	3	547	-365	-24	-16	994
1918	704	125	2	104	2	-3	4	632	-409	-27	-18	1,114
1919	808	112	2	106	2	-3	4	747	-463	-31	-20	1,262

Year												
1920	821	134	2	105	2	2	4	873	−504	−38	−22	1,375
1921	782	116	2	77	2	1	4	721	−441	−38	−19	1,205
1922	700	138	3	92	1	2	5	690	−422	−38	−18	1,153
1923	695	186	3	107	1	2	5	705	−441	−42	−19	1,202
1924	722	176	3	108	1	2	5	737	−453	−46	−20	1,235
1925	783	187	4	109	1	2	6	730	−470	−48	−21	1,283
1926	779	192	4	110	1	2	6	754	−476	−53	−21	1,298
1927	806	212	5	110	1	2	6	751	−488	−53	−21	1,331
1928	832	213	5	118	1	2	7	761	−499	−55	−22	1,363
1929	865	238	6	125	1	2	7	798	−526	−58	−23	1,436
1930	633	208	6	118	1	1	9	569	−515	−57	−20	952
1931	430	129	4	82	1	1	7	358	−406	−45	−11	548
1932	362	119	4	57	2	2	6	188	−276	−31	−9	421
1933	410	102	2	43	2	2	5	158	−195	−22	−7	498
1934	525	142	3	56	2	2	5	183	−242	−25	−8	640
1935	614	159	3	63	2	2	5	227	−288	−30	−10	744
1936	694	200	3	66	1	2	5	231	−327	−30	−7	836
1937	741	257	3	70	1	2	5	238	−362	−34	−10	909

1 A minus sign indicates that more rents and royalties are received by an industry than are paid. 2 Less than $500,000.

CHAPTER III

INDUSTRIAL SOURCES OF PRIVATE PRODUCTION INCOME

THE dynamic nature of the economy of the United States is perhaps nowhere better illustrated than in the sweeping adjustments which have taken place in the relative importance of the various industries as contributors to the national income in the past 140 years. While all forms of business were progressing and providing larger total incomes to those engaged in each of the various industries, their importance has undergone a series of fundamental changes as the United States developed from a group of agricultural colonies into a modern industrial nation.

The distribution of realized production income by industries is shown in Chart 7. Tables referred to follow the text of this.

In Colonial times agriculture and transportation were the dominant industries. At the beginning of the nineteenth century agriculture accounted for almost 40%, and transportation and communication for nearly 25%, of the total realized production income. Agriculture and transportation thus accounted for practically two-thirds of the income received by individuals in that period. Construction, comprising about 8% of the total income-yielding economic activity of the nation, occupied a more prominent place at that time than it has since; manufacturing was of minor importance.

By 1936 and 1937 manufacturing had preempted the position of major source of income, accounting for a fourth of the total. Agriculture and transportation had declined to a position of a little over 10% each, and were both exceeded in importance as a source of income by trade and service, as

48

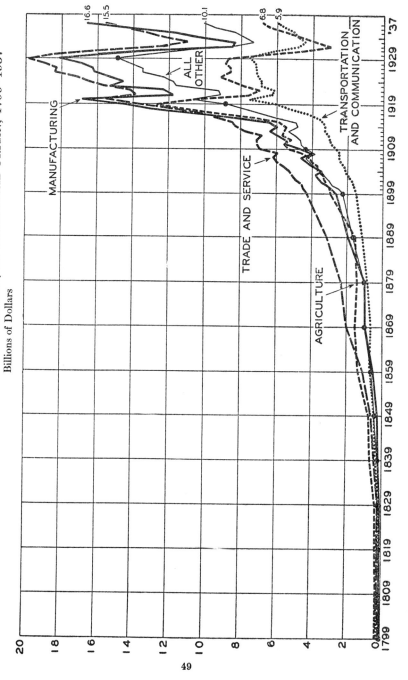

CHART 7: REALIZED PRIVATE PRODUCTION INCOME, BY INDUSTRIAL ORIGIN, 1799–1937

Billions of Dollars

MANUFACTURING

ALL OTHER

TRADE AND SERVICE

AGRICULTURE

TRANSPORTATION AND COMMUNICATION

16.6
15.5
10.1
6.8
5.9

20
18
16
14
12
10
8
6
4
2
0

1799 1809 1819 1829 1839 1849 1859 1869 1879 1889 1899 1909 1919 1929 '37

well as by manufacturing. The tremendous rise in the importance of government as a source of income distributed to individuals, from almost negligible proportions at the beginning of the nineteenth century to a prominent place in recent years, has already been mentioned.[1] Income derived from the regular government functions in the form of salaries and wages to regular employees and interest on government debt had also grown to a position of greater importance than either agriculture or transportation and communication in 1936 and 1937.

These striking shifts in relative importance of the various industries from the standpoint of the income they yield have not occurred uniformly as a steady progression, but have taken place very rapidly in some periods and then shown little change in the intervals between these dynamic eras. Agriculture, for example, showed little variation after a sharp decline in relative importance from 1799 to 1809, and maintained a proportion of between 30% and 34% of total income until the Civil War. A sharp drop then occurred to a new level of between 15% and 23%, which was maintained from 1879 until the World War. Another rapid decline then brought its contribution to total national income down to a level of between 12% and 16%; and this position prevailed from 1921 through 1929. During the subsequent depression there was a sharp drop and then a recovery in its relative importance.

Transportation and communication declined irregularly until the time of the Civil War and then dropped to a new level. These branches of industry have maintained a combined relative importance of between 11% and 14% for the past half century, showing very little change as a result of the World War.

On a par with the marked decline of agriculture as a source of income has been the spectacular increase in manufacturing.

[1] Pp. xiv, 19.

From an importance of under 5% at the turn of the nineteenth century, manufacturing increased to a position of 10% in 1829 and continued at about that level until 1859. By 1900 it accounted for about one-fifth of total private production income, this position being maintained until the World War, when it moved up to a new level of about 25%. This proportion has prevailed ever since, with some decline and recovery during the depression.

Mining and quarrying, electric light and power and gas production, which were of almost no importance as a source of income in 1799 now account for over 5% of the total.

AGRICULTURE

Agriculture is one of the few industries in which the small individual enterpriser is still dominant in the United States. Not only the management but a large part of the capital and a good part of the labor elements entering into production in this industry are supplied by the entrepreneur. As indicated in Tables 19 and 20, from two-thirds to nearly three-fourths of the income derived from this industry in recent years has been received by individual enterprisers.

Ordinarily, 20% or less of the income derived from agriculture is received by hired labor, and only about 10% is received by persons other than farm operators or labor. Many of these others are retired farmers or close relatives of the renters.[1] Interest on mortgages on the business portion of the farm property is also a comparatively small item in this industry, while the almost complete absence of the corporate form of enterprise explains why dividend income is negligible.

MINING AND QUARRYING

In the prosperity years of the 1920's, mining and quarrying accounted for $2.3 billion of the national income. They de-

[1] See R. F. Martin, "American Farm Tenancy Problems," National Industrial Conference Board, *Conference Board Bulletin*, November 30, 1937, pp. 122 ff.

clined during the recent depression to about $900 million but by 1936 had recovered to about $1.5 billion.

In contrast to the situation in agriculture, the independent enterpriser is of relatively small importance in mining and quarrying, and entrepreneurial income is therefore of little significance. Fixed debt likewise is not large, and the predominance of the corporate form of enterprise accounts for the fact that from 70% to 80% of the income derived from this industry (Tables 21, 22) is received in the form of salaries and wages, and, except in petroleum production, most of the remainder is returned in the form of dividends. Royalties paid to owners of mining properties, particularly petroleum deposits, have accounted for between 5% and 15% of the income total.

ELECTRIC LIGHT AND POWER AND GAS

The most rapidly growing major industry in this century, other than the automobile subdivision of manufacturing, has been the electric light and power utilities. Accounting for total income disbursements to individuals of only about $60 million at the turn of the century, this industry was thirty years later contributing $1.5 billion to the realized income total.

This industry is completely dominated by the corporate form of enterprise and requires a high proportion of fixed capital in relation to labor. Technological improvements since the turn of the century have increased the relative importance of the plant and equipment in relation to the labor requirement.

This situation and these developments requiring heavy investments are reflected in the distribution of income received from this industry. At the turn of this century 40% of the income total was accounted for by dividends and interest; by 1937 this proportion had increased to 56%. Salaries and wages, the only other type of income of any importance, have by 1937 this proportion had increased to 56%. The only other kind of income of any importance, salaries and wages, has declined in its share in the total income from 60% to just over 40% since 1900.

MANUFACTURING

Salaries and wages have in the past third of a century accounted for more than four-fifths of the income derived from the manufacturing industry, fluctuating between 80% and 87% in individual years.

The continued rise in the importance of the corporate form of enterprise, to the almost total exclusion of small individual enterprises in this industrial group, is reflected in the trend of entrepreneurial income and dividends since 1900. At that time dividends accounted for about 12% of the total realized income, and the net profits of individual enterprisers were about 6%. By 1929 and 1937 dividends had increased to about 15%, while entrepreneurial income had dropped to only 2% of the total.

Of special interest in this industry in recent years is the sudden increase in the relative share of dividends (see Table 26) in 1936, offset by a drop in the salary-and-wage proportion. This was brought about primarily by the provisions of the undistributed profits tax levied by the Federal Government, which forced out corporation earnings that might otherwise have been left for the use of business.

Interest and net rents and royalties are of negligible importance in manufacturing.

CONSTRUCTION

The construction industry classification used here includes only independent enterprises engaged principally in construction activity, and excludes all construction carried on for their own purposes by concerns primarily engaged in other industries.

This industry is organized chiefly into small independent contracting firms and individuals. Compared to these, the few extremely large and well-known contracting corporations are of relatively small importance, as shown by the kinds of income derived from this industry. Out of a total of $1.5 billion in 1937, about 82% was received in the form of salaries and wages, and 16% in the form of entrepreneurial income. The remaining 2% was distributed as dividends, interest and net rents and royalties, the bulk of it being in the form of dividends.

TRANSPORTATION

The various subdivisions of the transportation industry are organized on extremely diverse lines; railroads are, for example, practically all incorporated, whereas trucking and taxi services are conducted primarily by small unincorporated concerns or individuals.

Since 1900 the proportion of salaries and wages in the total income derived from transportation has increased from about two-thirds to over three-fourths of the total, while interest charges have been drastically reduced from a relative importance of about 20% to 8%. Most of this reduction came during the World War, when salaries and wages more than doubled, while interest increased only moderately. Dividend income in transportation declined from over 12% of the total before the World War to under 4% in 1920, primarily as a result of the railroad collapse after the extremely prosperous war years. The railroads were under emergency government management during the war period, but after this was terminated, the new proportions were maintained.

Interesting items which have arisen during the recent depression periods since 1929 have been the rapid increase in actual and relative importance of entrepreneurial income, brought about by a large increase in the number of small independent enterprisers entering the taxi and trucking business, and the rise and decline in the relative importance of interest, which is a stable type of income the actual amount of which did not decline greatly and recover, as was the case with the other kind of income in this period.

COMMUNICATION

One of the industries that has developed from very modest beginnings during the past third of a century into an important source of income is communication. By 1929 this industry was adding nearly a billion dollars a year to the income stream.

The high relative importance of capital investment in communications is reflected in the income derived from this source, about a fourth of which appeared in the form of dividends and interest. The remaining three-fourths has been accounted for by salaries and wages, since there are practically no small individual enterprisers in this industry.

TRADE

Trade is the second most important industry in the United States from the income-yielding standpoint, having surpassed agriculture in the years after the World War. It provided a total of over $11 billion in 1929 and over $8 billion in 1937.

In wholesale and retail trade, particularly the latter, there are still a great many independent enterprisers. Many of them rent the premises on which they do business. For these reasons entrepreneurial income and net rents and royalties provide an unusually large proportion of the total income received by individuals from this industry. Both of these have, however, been declining in relative importance as the corporate form of enterprise has continued to grow since 1900. At that time, the above types of income accounted for a third of the total, whereas in 1937 they provided only about 17%. At the same time salaries and wages have increased in importance from less than two-thirds of the total to more than three-fourths.

SERVICE INDUSTRIES

The service industrial classification includes several very different types of enterprises: the recreation and amusements pursuits; business and personal services, such as repair shops and hotels; professional services, such as those of doctors and lawyers; and domestic service. This industry accounted for over $8 billion of the national income total in 1929.

Practically all the income received from this industry is in the form of salaries and wages and entrepreneurial income, with about two-thirds in the former category and one-third in the latter. The large proportion of entrepreneurial income is accounted for by the inclusion in this industrial classification of professional practitioners, such as doctors and lawyers, and a large number of independent service establishment proprietors.

FINANCE

The financial classification of industries provided about $3 billion of the total income received by individuals in 1929 and about $1.7 billion in 1937. This industry is conducted almost entirely by incorporated enterprises. (Brokerage and similar activities have been included in the miscellaneous industry classification.)

Financial organizations receive more income in the form of net rents and royalties than they disburse in this form. Hence this item is shown as a negative quantity in these estimates, and no percentage distribution by kind of income for this industry is shown. As can be seen from Table 37, however, salaries and wages in recent years have accounted for as much as ten times as much of the income derived from this source as did dividends.

A striking development in recent years in this industry has been the downward trend of interest on long-term debt disbursed in comparison with the amount received. Declining interest rates, brought about partly by governmental activities and partly by a decline in outstanding debt through both involuntary liquidation and voluntary curtailment, has been responsible for a shift from a larger proportion of interest disbursed by the finance industry to a greater proportion received. Interest appeared as a negative item in finance beginning in 1935.

Miscellaneous

The miscellaneous classification includes income received by self-employed persons engaged in the hand trades such as cabinet making and dressmaking, in fishing, in brokerage activities and in miscellaneous professional occupations such as the clergy. It includes also an estimate for salaries and wages received by employed persons not covered in other classifications.

The dividends, interest and rents and royalties are those reported by corporations in the miscellaneous industrial classification. It will be noted that more dividends were reported received than paid by corporations in this group in three different years, and more net rents and royalties were reported received than paid in all years.

It is apparent from the above that this is distinctly a catch-all classification. These estimates are among the least satisfactory in the national income total, and no great reliance should be placed upon the estimates of the total and individual types as reflecting the volume or trend of any one of the heterogeneous components above mentioned.

TABLE 16: REALIZED PRIVATE PRODUCTION INCOME, BY INDUSTRIES, 1799–1937

Millions of Dollars

Year	Agriculture	Mining and Quarrying	Electric Light and Power and Gas	Manufacturing	Construction	Transportation and Communication	Trade	Service	Miscellaneous[1]		Total, Private Production Income
									Finance	Other	
1799	264	1	2	32	53	160	35	64		59	668
1809	306	2	2	55	72	236	41	110		79	901
1819	294	2	2	64	58	176	55	132		74	855
1829	329	3	2	98	66	143	61	163		84	947
1839	545	5	1	162	95	277	135	222		135	1,577
1849	737	16	2	291	133	398	196	355		198	2,326
1859	1,264	44	6	495	184	694	494	572		345	4,098
1869	1,517	102	23	1,000	387	718	1,039	968		534	6,288
1879	1,371	153	33	960	360	896	1,166	1,099		579	6,617
1889	1,517	232	44	2,022	631	1,154	1,803	1,341		834	9,578
1899	2,933	416	58	2,714	655	1,528	2,578	1,745	196	1,013	13,836
1900	3,034	453	65	2,941	627	1,626	2,720	1,774	233	1,077	14,550
1901	3,153	552	75	3,193	758	1,720	2,858	1,786	290	1,152	15,587
1902	3,335	494	77	3,605	839	1,820	3,098	1,820	372	1,245	16,705
1903	3,439	671	89	3,812	852	1,968	3,272	1,869	404	1,315	17,691
1904	3,708	645	99	3,519	919	2,081	3,380	1,904	469	1,335	18,059
1905	3,678	746	103	4,032	1,052	2,210	3,692	1,939	474	1,437	19,363
1906	4,029	835	120	4,377	1,183	2,431	4,019	1,973	474	1,567	21,008
1907	4,214	1,049	134	4,743	1,096	2,544	4,168	2,064	433	1,667	22,112
1908	4,621	771	139	4,046	888	2,524	3,894	2,113	469	1,584	21,049
1909	5,311	859	157	4,824	1,153	2,648	4,310	2,544	492	1,735	24,033
1910	5,563	949	168	5,447	1,136	2,853	4,496	2,557	544	1,856	25,569
1911	5,241	949	192	5,458	1,108	2,945	4,548	2,514	596	1,834	25,385
1912	5,679	1,039	211	5,996	1,224	3,106	4,425	2,371	657	1,851	26,559
1913	5,559	1,183	228	6,415	1,312	3,260	5,081	2,692	686	1,975	28,391
1914	5,518	1,008	250	6,012	980	3,248	5,508	2,832	682	1,916	27,954

Year											
1915	5,921	1,016	268	6,401	976	3,346	5,677	2,837	717	1,955	29,114
1916	7,072	1,452	299	8,747	1,080	3,727	6,290	3,039	792	2,604	35,032
1917	9,590	1,773	332	10,843	1,056	4,269	6,978	3,357	850	2,966	42,014
1918	11,595	2,019	373	13,076	1,132	5,410	7,842	3,830	952	3,291	49,520
1919	12,699	1,910	429	14,340	1,633	6,089	9,177	4,465	1,233	3,564	55,539
1920	10,569	2,628	480	16,811	2,224	7,474	10,048	5,436	1,488	3,837	60,995
1921	7,569	1,982	500	11,759	1,720	6,282	8,511	5,422	1,625	3,393	48,763
1922	7,087	1,845	569	12,303	2,092	6,217	8,831	5,366	1,664	3,112	49,036
1923	7,907	2,613	715	15,285	2,824	6,808	9,725	5,929	1,878	3,529	57,213
1924	8,526	2,276	854	14,591	2,874	6,800	9,977	6,468	2,062	3,750	58,178
1925	9,048	2,243	937	15,410	3,023	6,978	10,405	6,777	2,272	3,856	60,949
1926	8,614	2,573	1,036	16,186	3,144	7,191	10,878	7,508	2,454	4,273	63,857
1927	8,599	2,322	1,117	16,282	3,096	7,243	10,709	7,600	2,615	4,359	63,942
1928	8,756	2,098	1,261	16,920	3,257	7,166	10,874	7,951	2,900	4,470	65,653
1929	8,720	2,295	1,392	18,059	3,225	7,451	11,446	8,378	3,198	4,706	68,872
1930	6,761	1,918	1,559	15,958	2,910	7,012	10,628	7,889	2,963	4,371	61,968
1931	4,476	1,323	1,478	12,376	1,945	6,049	9,126	6,889	2,719	3,684	50,066
1932	3,040	929	1,339	8,528	932	4,807	6,992	5,409	2,204	2,952	37,132
1933	3,771	902	1,156	8,428	762	4,445	6,132	4,893	1,838	2,744	35,074
1934	4,661	1,172	1,143	10,471	928	4,790	6,853	5,404	1,787	2,996	40,205
1935	5,517	1,243	1,158	11,720	1,043	5,110	7,309	6,016	1,692	3,226	44,037
1936	6,378	1,481	1,212	14,138	1,447	5,605	7,704	6,658	1,597	3,632	49,852
1937	6,757	1,743	1,264	16,629	1,806	5,934	8,414	7,130	1,674	3,608	54,959

[1] Miscellaneous, including Finance, prior to 1899.

[2] Less than $500,000.

TABLE 17: PERCENTAGE DISTRIBUTION OF REALIZED PRIVATE PRODUCTION INCOME, BY INDUSTRIES, 1799–1937

Year	Agriculture	Mining and Quarrying	Electric Light and Power and Gas	Manufacturing	Construction	Transportation and Communication	Trade	Service	Miscellaneous[1]	
									Finance	Other
1799	39.5	0.1	[2]	4.8	7.9	24.0	5.2	9.6		8.8
1809	34.0	0.2	[2]	6.1	8.0	26.2	4.6	12.2		8.8
1819	34.4	0.2	[2]	7.5	6.8	20.6	6.4	15.4		8.7
1829	34.7	0.3	[2]	10.3	7.0	15.1	6.4	17.2		8.9
1839	34.6	0.3	0.1	10.3	6.0	17.6	8.6	14.1		8.6
1849	31.7	0.7	0.1	12.5	5.7	17.1	8.4	15.3		8.5
1859	30.8	1.1	0.1	12.1	4.5	16.9	12.1	14.0		8.4
1869	24.1	1.6	0.4	15.9	6.2	11.4	16.5	15.4		8.5
1879	20.7	2.3	0.5	14.5	5.4	13.5	17.6	16.6		8.8
1889	15.8	2.4	0.5	21.1	6.6	12.0	18.8	14.0		8.7
1899	21.2	3.0	0.4	19.6	4.7	11.0	18.6	12.6	1.4	7.3
1900	20.9	3.1	0.4	20.2	4.3	11.2	18.7	12.2	1.6	7.4
1901	20.3	3.6	0.5	20.6	4.9	11.1	18.4	11.5	1.9	7.4
1902	20.0	3.0	0.5	21.6	5.0	10.9	18.5	10.9	2.2	7.5
1903	19.4	3.8	0.5	21.5	4.8	11.1	18.5	10.6	2.3	7.4
1904	20.5	3.6	0.5	19.5	5.1	11.5	18.7	10.5	2.6	7.4
1905	19.0	3.9	0.5	20.8	5.4	11.4	19.1	10.0	2.4	7.4
1906	19.2	4.0	0.6	20.8	5.6	11.6	19.1	9.4	2.3	7.5
1907	19.1	4.7	0.6	21.4	5.0	11.5	18.8	9.3	2.0	7.5
1908	22.0	3.7	0.7	19.2	4.2	12.0	18.5	10.0	2.2	7.5
1909	22.1	3.6	0.7	20.1	4.8	11.0	17.9	10.6	2.0	7.2
1910	21.8	3.7	0.7	21.3	4.4	11.2	17.6	10.0	2.1	7.3
1911	20.6	3.7	0.8	21.5	4.4	11.6	17.9	9.9	2.3	7.2
1912	21.4	3.9	0.8	22.6	4.6	11.7	16.7	8.9	2.5	7.0
1913	19.6	4.2	0.8	22.6	4.6	11.5	17.9	9.5	2.4	7.0
1914	19.7	3.6	0.9	21.5	3.5	11.6	19.7	10.1	2.4	6.9

Year										
1915	20.3	3.5	0.9	22.0	3.4	11.5	19.5	9.7	2.5	6.7
1916	20.2	4.1	0.9	25.0	3.1	10.6	17.8	8.7	2.3	7.4
1917	22.8	4.2	0.8	25.8	2.5	10.2	16.6	8.0	2.0	7.1
1918	23.4	4.1	0.8	26.4	2.3	10.9	15.8	7.7	1.9	6.6
1919	22.9	3.4	0.8	25.8	2.9	11.0	16.5	8.0	2.2	6.4
1920	17.3	4.3	0.8	27.6	3.6	12.3	16.5	8.9	2.4	6.3
1921	15.5	4.1	1.0	24.1	3.5	12.9	17.5	11.1	3.3	7.0
1922	14.4	3.8	1.2	25.1	4.3	12.7	18.0	10.9	3.4	6.3
1923	13.8	4.6	1.2	26.7	4.9	11.9	17.0	10.4	3.3	6.2
1924	14.7	3.9	1.5	25.1	4.9	11.7	17.1	11.1	3.5	6.4
1925	14.8	3.7	1.5	25.3	5.0	11.4	17.1	11.1	3.7	6.3
1926	13.5	4.0	1.6	25.3	4.9	11.3	17.0	11.8	3.8	6.7
1927	13.4	3.6	1.7	25.5	4.8	11.3	16.7	11.9	4.1	6.8
1928	13.3	3.2	1.9	25.8	5.0	10.9	16.6	12.1	4.4	6.8
1929	12.7	3.3	2.0	26.2	4.7	10.8	16.6	12.2	4.6	6.8
1930	10.9	3.1	2.5	25.8	4.7	11.3	17.2	12.7	4.8	7.1
1931	8.9	2.6	3.0	24.7	3.9	12.1	18.3	13.8	5.4	7.4
1932	8.2	2.5	3.6	23.0	2.5	12.9	18.8	14.6	5.9	8.0
1933	10.8	2.6	3.3	24.0	2.2	12.7	17.5	14.0	5.2	7.8
1934	11.6	2.9	2.8	26.0	2.3	11.9	17.0	13.4	4.4	7.5
1935	12.5	2.8	2.6	26.6	2.4	11.6	16.6	13.7	3.8	7.3
1936	12.8	3.0	2.4	28.4	2.9	11.2	15.5	13.4	3.2	7.3
1937	12.3	3.2	2.3	30.3	3.3	10.8	15.3	13.0	3.0	6.6

[1] Miscellaneous, including Finance, prior to 1899.
[2] Less than $500,000.

TABLE 18: INDEXES OF REALIZED PRIVATE PRODUCTION INCOME, BY INDUSTRIES, 1799–1937

1929 = 100

Year	Agriculture	Mining and Quarrying	Electric Light and Power and Gas	Manufacturing	Construction	Transportation and Communication	Trade	Service	Miscellaneous		Total, Private Production Income
									Finance	Other	
1799	3.0	1	1	0.2	1.6	2.1	0.3	0.8	0.7		1.0
1809	3.5	0.1	1	0.3	2.2	3.2	0.4	1.3	1.0		1.3
1819	3.4	0.1	1	0.4	1.8	2.4	0.5	1.6	0.9		1.2
1829	3.8	0.1	1	0.5	2.0	1.9	0.5	1.9	1.1		1.4
1839	6.3	0.2	0.1	0.9	2.9	3.7	1.2	2.6	1.7		2.3
1849	8.5	0.7	0.1	1.6	4.1	5.3	1.7	4.2	2.5		3.4
1859	14.5	1.9	0.4	2.7	5.7	9.3	4.3	6.8	4.4		6.0
1869	17.4	4.4	1.7	5.5	12.0	9.6	9.1	11.6	6.8		9.1
1879	15.7	6.7	2.4	5.3	11.2	12.0	10.2	13.1	7.3		9.6
1889	17.4	10.1	3.2	11.2	19.6	15.5	15.8	16.0	10.6		13.9
1899	33.6	18.1	4.2	15.0	20.3	20.5	22.5	20.8	6.1	21.5	20.1
1900	34.8	19.7	4.7	16.3	19.4	21.8	23.8	21.2	7.3	22.9	21.1
1901	36.2	24.1	5.4	17.7	23.5	23.1	25.0	21.3	9.1	24.5	22.6
1902	38.2	21.5	5.5	20.0	26.0	24.4	27.1	21.7	11.6	26.5	24.3
1903	39.4	29.2	6.4	21.1	26.4	26.4	28.6	22.3	12.6	27.9	25.7
1904	42.5	28.1	7.1	19.5	28.5	27.9	29.5	22.7	14.7	28.4	26.2
1905	42.2	32.5	7.4	22.3	32.6	29.7	32.3	23.1	14.8	30.5	28.1
1906	46.2	36.4	8.6	24.2	36.7	32.6	35.1	23.5	14.8	33.3	30.5
1907	48.3	45.7	9.6	26.3	34.0	34.1	36.4	24.6	13.5	35.4	32.1
1908	53.0	33.6	10.0	22.4	27.5	33.9	34.0	25.2	14.7	33.7	30.6
1909	60.9	37.4	11.3	26.7	35.8	35.5	37.7	30.4	15.4	36.9	34.9
1910	63.8	41.4	12.1	30.2	35.2	38.3	39.3	30.5	17.0	39.4	37.1
1911	60.1	41.4	13.8	30.2	34.4	39.5	39.7	30.0	18.6	39.0	36.9
1912	65.1	45.3	15.2	33.2	38.0	41.7	38.7	28.3	20.5	39.3	38.6
1913	63.8	51.5	16.4	35.5	40.7	43.8	44.4	32.1	21.5	42.0	41.2
1914	63.3	43.9	18.0	33.3	30.4	43.6	48.1	33.8	21.3	40.7	40.6

Year											
1915	67.9	44.3	19.3	35.4	30.3	44.9	49.6	33.9	22.4	41.5	42.3
1916	81.1	63.3	21.5	48.4	33.5	50.0	54.3	36.3	24.8	55.3	50.9
1917	110.0	77.3	23.9	60.0	32.7	57.3	61.0	40.1	26.6	63.0	61.0
1918	133.0	88.0	26.8	72.4	35.1	72.6	68.5	45.7	29.8	69.9	71.9
1919	145.6	83.2	30.8	79.4	50.6	81.7	80.2	53.3	38.6	75.7	80.6
1920	121.2	114.5	34.5	93.1	69.0	100.3	87.8	64.9	46.5	81.5	88.6
1921	56.8	86.4	35.9	65.1	53.3	84.3	74.4	64.7	50.8	72.1	70.8
1922	30.7	80.4	40.9	68.1	64.9	83.4	77.2	64.0	52.0	66.1	71.2
1923	90.7	113.9	51.4	84.6	87.6	91.4	85.0	70.8	58.7	75.0	83.1
1924	97.8	99.2	61.4	80.8	89.1	91.3	87.2	77.2	64.5	79.7	84.5
1925	103.8	97.7	67.3	85.3	93.7	93.7	90.9	80.9	71.0	81.9	88.5
1926	98.8	112.1	74.4	89.6	97.5	96.5	95.0	89.6	76.7	90.8	92.7
1927	98.6	101.2	80.2	90.2	96.0	97.2	93.6	90.7	81.8	92.6	92.8
1928	100.4	91.4	90.6	93.7	101.0	96.2	95.0	94.9	90.7	95.0	95.3
1929	100.0	100.0	100.0	100.0	100.0	100.0	100.0	100.0	100.0	100.0	100.0
1930	77.5	83.6	112.0	88.4	90.2	94.1	92.9	94.2	92.7	92.9	90.0
1931	51.3	57.6	106.2	68.5	60.3	81.2	79.7	82.2	85.0	78.3	72.7
1932	34.9	40.5	96.2	47.2	28.9	64.5	61.1	64.6	68.9	62.7	53.9
1933	43.2	39.3	83.0	46.7	23.6	59.7	53.6	58.4	57.5	58.3	50.9
1934	53.5	51.1	82.1	58.0	28.8	64.3	59.9	64.5	55.9	63.7	58.4
1935	63.3	54.2	83.2	64.9	32.3	68.6	63.9	71.8	52.9	68.6	63.9
1936	73.1	64.5	87.1	78.3	44.9	75.2	67.3	79.5	49.9	77.2	72.4
1937	77.5	75.9	90.8	92.1	56.0	79.6	73.5	85.1	52.3	76.7	79.8

¹ Less than 0.05 per cent.

63

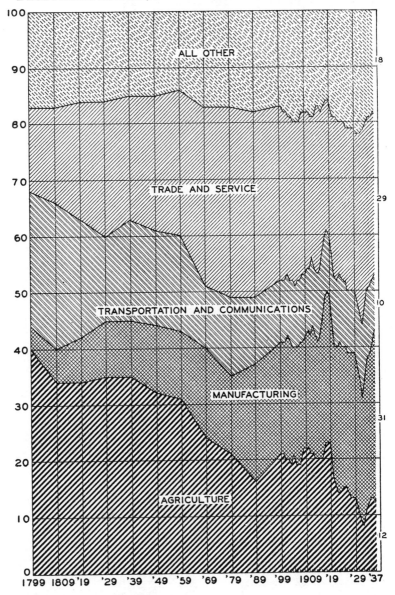

TABLE 19: REALIZED INCOME FROM AGRICULTURE, BY KIND, 1899–1937

Millions of Dollars

Year	Salaries and Wages	Entrepreneurial Income	Dividends	Interest	Net Rents and Royalties	Total, All Types
1899	459	2,125	11	114	224	2,933
1900	526	2,150	8	113	237	3,034
1901	524	2,250	13	122	244	3,153
1902	590	2,350	9	131	255	3,335
1903	615	2,400	8	139	277	3,439
1904	717	2,550	10	146	285	3,708
1905	716	2,500	15	153	294	3,678
1906	827	2,700	23	159	320	4,029
1907	823	2,850	29	164	348	4,214
1908	867	3,200	18	170	366	4,621
1909	855	3,831	18	174	433	5,311
1910	853	4,044	20	184	462	5,563
1911	896	3,638	17	194	496	5,241
1912	900	4,073	21	203	482	5,679
1913	925	3,899	28	210	497	5,559
1914	901	3,870	20	221	506	5,518
1915	921	4,228	19	236	517	5,921
1916	987	5,215	49	262	559	7,072
1917	1,229	7,372	56	302	631	9,590
1918	1,447	9,046	47	351	704	11,595
1919	1,778	9,675	27	411	808	12,699
1920	2,042	7,211	29	466	821	10,569
1921	1,307	4,980	27	473	782	7,569
1922	1,272	4,562	19	484	700	7,037
1923	1,440	5,269	20	483	695	7,907
1924	1,418	5,884	19	483	722	8,526
1925	1,473	6,284	22	486	783	9,048
1926	1,527	5,803	20	485	779	8,614
1927	1,543	5,722	32	496	806	8,599
1928	1,554	5,843	33	494	832	8,756
1929	1,565	5,797	20	473	865	8,720
1930	1,322	4,372	13	422	633	6,761
1931	957	2,720	17	352	430	4,476
1932	619	1,758	6	294	362	3,040
1933	574	2,485	1	303	410	3,771
1934	615	3,224	17	279	526	4,661
1935	656	3,958	20	269	614	5,517
1936	768	4,616	23	277	694	6,378
1937	879	4,839	25	273	741	6,757

[1] Less than $500,000.

TABLE 20: PERCENTAGE DISTRIBUTION OF REALIZED INCOME FROM AGRICULTURE, BY KIND, 1899–1937

Year	Salaries and Wages	Entrepreneurial Income	Dividends	Interest	Net Rents and Royalties
1899	15.6	72.5	0.4	3.9	7.6
1900	17.3	70.9	0.3	3.7	7.8
1901	16.6	71.4	0.4	3.9	7.7
1902	17.7	70.5	0.3	3.9	7.6
1903	17.9	69.8	0.2	4.0	8.1
1904	19.3	68.8	0.3	3.9	7.7
1905	19.5	68.0	0.4	4.2	8.0
1906	20.5	67.0	0.6	3.9	7.9
1907	19.5	67.6	0.7	3.9	8.3
1908	18.8	69.2	0.4	3.7	7.9
1909	16.1	72.1	0.3	3.3	8.2
1910	15.3	72.7	0.4	3.3	8.3
1911	17.1	69.4	0.3	3.7	9.5
1912	15.8	71.7	0.4	3.6	8.5
1913	16.6	70.1	0.5	3.8	· 8.9
1914	16.3	70.1	0.4	4.0	9.2
1915	15.6	71.4	0.3	4.0	8.7
1916	14.0	73.7	0.7	3.7	7.9
1917	12.8	76.9	0.6	3.1	6.6
1918	12.5	78.0	0.4	3.0	6.1
1919	14.0	76.2	0.2	3.2	6.4
1920	19.3	68.2	0.3	4.4	7.8
1921	17.3	65.8	0.4	6.2	10.3
1922	18.1	64.8	0.3	6.9	9.9
1923	18.2	66.6	0.3	6.1	8.8
1924	16.6	69.0	0.2	5.7	8.5
1925	16.3	69.5	0.2	5.4	8.7
1926	17.7	67.4	0.2	5.6	9.0
1927	17.9	66.5	0.4	5.8	9.4
1928	17.7	66.7	0.4	5.6	9.5
1929	17.9	66.5	0.2	5.4	9.9
1930	19.6	64.7	0.2	6.2	9.4
1931	21.4	60.8	0.4	7.9	9.6
1932	20.4	57.8	0.2	9.7	11.9
1933	15.2	65.9	0.1	8.0	10.9
1934	13.2	69.2	0.4	6.0	11.3
1935	11.9	71.7	0.4	4.9	11.1
1936	12.0	72.4	0.4	4.3	10.9
1937	13.0	71.6	0.4	4.0	11.0

TABLE 21: REALIZED INCOME FROM MINING AND QUARRYING, BY KIND, 1899–1937

Millions of Dollars

Year	Salaries and Wages	Entrepreneurial Income	Dividends	Interest	Net Rents and Royalties	Total, All Types
1899	289	17	79	5	26	416
1900	344	19	57	5	28	453
1901	405	20	91	6	30	552
1902	371	18	64	6	35	494
1903	545	21	59	7	39	671
1904	509	20	67	8	41	645
1905	561	20	109	8	48	746
1906	592	20	163	9	51	835
1907	754	21	204	10	60	1,049
1908	565	18	123	10	55	771
1909	643	18	127	11	60	859
1910	709	20	142	12	66	949
1911	725	20	124	13	67	949
1912	784	21	148	14	72	1,039
1913	867	23	200	15	78	1,183
1914	752	21	142	16	77	1,008
1915	758	21	135	17	85	1,016
1916	953	28	349	19	103	1,452
1917	1,195	35	404	20	119	1,773
1918	1,489	45	338	22	125	2,019
1919	1,532	46	195	25	112	1,910
1920	2,192	59	210	33	134	2,628
1921	1,582	49	193	42	116	1,982
1922	1,485	47	139	36	138	1,845
1923	2,111	52	223	41	186	2,613
1924	1,787	44	213	56	176	2,276
1925	1,687	41	269	59	187	2,243
1926	1,963	40	327	51	192	2,573
1927	1,746	38	278	48	212	2,322
1928	1,551	35	253	46	213	2,098
1929	1,614	32	365	46	238	2,295
1930	1,386	34	249	41	208	1,918
1931	978	35	138	43	129	1,323
1932	658	34	82	37	119	929
1933	658	31	75	36	102	902
1934	857	32	107	34	142	1,172
1935	901	33	118	33	159	1,243
1936	1,032	36	178	35	200	1,481
1937	1,167	39	243	37	257	1,743

TABLE 22: PERCENTAGE DISTRIBUTION OF REALIZED INCOME FROM MINING AND QUARRYING, BY KIND, 1899–1937

Year	Salaries and Wages	Entrepreneurial Income	Dividends	Interest	Net Rents and Royalties
1899	69.5	4.1	19.0	1.2	6.2
1900	75.9	4.2	12.6	1.1	6.2
1901	73.4	3.6	16.5	1.1	5.4
1902	75.1	3.6	13.0	1.2	7.1
1903	81.2	3.1	8.8	1.0	5.8
1904	78.9	3.1	10.4	1.2	6.4
1905	75.2	2.7	14.6	1.1	6.4
1906	70.9	2.4	19.5	1.1	6.1
1907	71.9	2.0	19.4	1.0	5.7
1908	73.3	2.3	16.0	1.3	7.1
1909	74.9	2.1	14.8	1.3	7.0
1910	74.7	2.1	15.0	1.3	7.0
1911	76.4	2.1	13.1	1.4	7.1
1912	75.5	2.0	14.2	1.3	6.9
1913	73.3	1.9	16.9	1.3	6.6
1914	74.6	2.1	14.1	1.6	7.6
1915	74.6	2.1	13.3	1.7	8.4
1916	65.6	1.9	24.0	1.3	7.1
1917	67.4	2.0	22.8	1.1	6.7
1918	73.7	2.2	16.7	1.1	6.2
1919	80.2	2.4	10.2	1.3	5.9
1920	83.4	2.2	8.0	1.3	5.1
1921	79.8	2.5	9.7	2.1	5.9
1922	80.5	2.5	7.5	2.0	7.5
1923	80.8	2.0	8.5	1.6	7.1
1924	78.5	1.9	9.4	2.5	7.7
1925	75.2	1.8	12.0	2.6	8.3
1926	76.2	1.6	12.7	2.0	7.5
1927	75.2	1.6	12.0	2.1	9.1
1928	73.9	1.7	12.1	2.2	10.2
1929	70.3	1.4	15.9	2.0	10.4
1930	72.3	1.8	13.0	2.1	10.8
1931	73.9	2.6	10.4	3.3	9.8
1932	70.8	3.7	8.8	4.0	12.8
1933	72.9	3.4	8.3	4.0	11.3
1934	73.1	2.7	9.1	2.9	12.1
1935	72.5	2.7	9.5	2.7	12.8
1936	69.7	2.4	12.0	2.4	13.5
1937	67.0	2.2	13.9	2.1	14.7

TABLE 23: REALIZED INCOME FROM ELECTRIC LIGHT AND POWER AND GAS, BY KIND, 1899-1937

Millions of Dollars

Year	Salaries and Wages	Dividends	Interest	Net Rents and Royalties	Total, All Types
1899	35	10	13	1	58
1900	41	11	13	1	65
1901	47	12	16	1	75
1902	46	13	18	1	77
1903	52	15	22	1	89
1904	56	17	26	1	99
1905	56	19	28	1	103
1906	66	21	33	1	120
1907	74	24	36	1	134
1908	76	23	39	1	139
1909	86	28	42	1	157
1910	96	30	41	1	168
1911	104	37	50	1	192
1912	116	41	53	1	211
1913	126	44	57	1	228
1914	135	54	59	2	250
1915	142	60	64	2	268
1916	160	67	70	2	299
1917	176	74	80	2	332
1918	190	83	98	2	373
1919	232	90	105	2	429
1920	275	89	114	2	480
1921	282	90	126	2	500
1922	300	120	146	3	569
1923	373	161	178	3	715
1924	439	194	218	3	854
1925	457	230	246	4	937
1926	503	243	286	4	1,036
1927	526	273	313	5	1,117
1928	565	346	345	5	1,261
1929	616	413	358	6	1,392
1930	609	565	379	6	1,559
1931	543	506	425	4	1,478
1932	440	449	447	4	1,339
1933	398	324	431	2	1,156
1934	440	272	429	3	1,143
1935	467	270	419	3	1,158
1936	508	305	396	3	1,212
1937	556	336	369	3	1,264

[1] Less than $500,000.

Table 24: Percentage Distribution of Realized-Income from Electric Light and Power and Gas, by Kind, 1899–1937

Year	Salaries and Wages	Dividends	Interest	Net Rents and Royalties
1899	60.3	17.2	22.4	1
1900	63.1	16.9	20.0	1
1901	62.7	16.0	21.3	1
1902	59.7	16.9	23.4	1
1903	58.4	16.9	24.7	1
1904	56.6	17.2	26.3	1
1905	54.4	18.4	27.2	1
1906	55.0	17.5	27.5	1
1907	55.2	17.9	26.9	1
1908	54.7	16.5	28.1	0.7
1909	54.8	17.8	26.8	0.6
1910	57.1	17.9	24.4	0.6
1911	54.2	19.3	26.0	0.5
1912	55.0	19.4	25.1	0.5
1913	55.3	19.3	25.0	0.4
1914	54.0	21.6	23.6	0.8
1915	53.0	22.4	23.9	0.7
1916	53.5	22.4	23.4	0.7
1917	53.0	22.3	24.1	0.6
1918	50.9	22.3	26.3	0.5
1919	54.1	21.0	24.5	0.5
1920	57.3	18.5	23.7	0.4
1921	56.4	18.0	25.2	0.4
1922	52.7	21.1	25.7	0.5
1923	52.2	22.5	24.9	0.4
1924	51.4	22.7	25.5	0.4
1925	48.8	24.5	26.3	0.4
1926	48.6	23.5	27.6	0.4
1927	47.1	24.4	28.0	0.4
1928	44.8	27.4	27.4	0.4
1929	44.3	29.7	25.7	0.4
1930	39.1	36.2	24.3	0.4
1931	36.7	34.2	28.8	0.3
1932	32.9	33.5	33.4	0.3
1933	34.4	28.0	37.3	0.2
1934	38.5	23.8	37.5	0.3
1935	40.3	23.3	36.2	0.3
1936	41.9	25.2	32.7	0.2
1937	44.0	26.6	29.2	0.2

[1] Less than 0.05%.

TABLE 25: REALIZED INCOME FROM MANUFACTURING, BY KIND, 1899–1937

Millions of Dollars

Year	Salaries and Wages	Entrepreneurial Income	Dividends	Interest	Net Rents and Royalties	Total, All Types
1899	2,181	172	285	47	29	2,714
1900	2,321	179	357	52	32	2,941
1901	2,548	191	369	53	32	3,193
1902	2,871	211	433	55	35	3,605
1903	3,083	223	413	57	36	3,812
1904	2,891	206	327	58	37	3,519
1905	3,362	238	333	60	39	4,032
1906	3,633	256	383	62	43	4,377
1907	3,928	275	429	64	47	4,743
1908	3,286	229	419	65	47	4,046
1909	3,988	277	439	67	53	4,824
1910	4,507	300	519	68	53	5,447
1911	4,482	291	563	69	53	5,458
1912	4,964	312	598	70	52	5,996
1913	5,310	325	656	72	52	6,415
1914	4,964	296	628	73	51	6,012
1915	5,310	296	668	75	52	6,401
1916	7,051	356	1,198	77	65	8,747
1917	8,866	419	1,383	79	96	10,843
1918	11,076	500	1,315	81	104	13,076
1919	12,348	539	1,262	85	106	14,340
1920	14,563	548	1,488	107	105	16,811
1921	9,793	428	1,324	137	77	11,759
1922	10,369	426	1,311	105	92	12,303
1923	12,894	406	1,761	117	107	15,285
1924	12,274	404	1,651	154	108	14,591
1925	12,835	406	1,908	152	109	15,410
1926	13,411	397	2,117	151	110	16,186
1927	13,411	384	2,225	152	110	16,282
1928	13,786	378	2,505	183	118	16,920
1929	14,770	378	2,575	210	125	18,059
1930	12,661	323	2,613	244	118	15,958
1931	9,901	274	1,894	225	82	12,376
1932	7,008	156	1,116	192	57	8,528
1933	7,045	159	1,009	172	43	8,428
1934	8,815	184	1,255	161	56	10,471
1935	9,890	196	1,421	149	63	11,720
1936	11,425	276	2,239	132	66	14,138
1937	13,614	329	2,508	108	70	16,629

TABLE 26: PERCENTAGE DISTRIBUTION OF REALIZED INCOME FROM MANUFACTURING, BY KIND, 1899–1937

Year	Salaries and Wages	Entrepreneurial Income	Dividends	Interest	Net Rents and Royalties
1899	80.4	6.3	10.5	1.7	1.1
1900	78.9	6.1	12.1	1.8	1.1
1901	79.8	6.0	11.6	1.7	1.0
1902	79.6	5.9	12.0	1.5	1.0
1903	80.9	5.8	10.8	1.5	0.9
1904	82.2	5.9	9.3	1.6	1.1
1905	83.4	5.9	8.3	1.5	1.0
1906	83.0	5.8	8.8	1.4	1.0
1907	82.8	5.8	9.0	1.3	1.0
1908	81.2	5.7	10.4	1.6	1.2
1909	82.7	5.7	9.1	1.4	1.1
1910	82.7	5.5	9.5	1.2	1.0
1911	82.1	5.3	10.3	1.3	1.0
1912	82.8	5.2	10.0	1.2	0.9
1913	82.8	5.1	10.2	1.1	0.8
1914	82.6	4.9	10.4	1.2	0.8
1915	83.0	4.6	10.4	1.2	0.8
1916	80.6	4.1	13.7	0.9	0.7
1917	81.8	3.9	12.8	0.7	0.9
1918	84.7	3.8	10.1	0.6	0.8
1919	86.1	3.8	8.8	0.6	0.7
1920	86.6	3.3	8.9	0.6	0.6
1921	83.3	3.6	11.3	1.2	0.7
1922	84.3	3.5	10.7	0.9	0.7
1923	84.4	2.7	11.5	0.8	0.7
1924	84.1	2.8	11.3	1.1	0.7
1925	83.3	2.6	12.4	1.0	0.7
1926	82.9	2.5	13.1	0.9	0.7
1927	82.4	2.4	13.7	0.9	0.7
1928	81.2	2.2	14.8	1.1	0.7
1929	81.8	2.1	14.3	1.2	0.7
1930	79.3	2.0	16.4	1.5	0.7
1931	80.0	2.2	15.3	1.8	0.7
1932	82.2	1.8	13.1	2.3	0.7
1933	83.6	1.9	12.0	2.0	0.5
1934	84.2	1.8	12.0	1.5	0.5
1935	84.4	1.7	12.1	1.3	0.5
1936	80.8	2.0	15.8	0.9	0.5
1937	81.9	2.0	15.1	0.6	0.5

TABLE 27: REALIZED INCOME FROM CONSTRUCTION, BY KIND, 1899–1937

Millions of Dollars

Year	Salaries and Wages	Entrepreneurial Income	Dividends	Interest	Net Rents and Royalties	Total, All Types
1899	531	116	6	2	..	655
1900	508	111	6	2	..	627
1901	616	134	6	2	..	758
1902	682	149	6	2	..	839
1903	692	151	7	2	..	852
1904	748	163	5	3	..	919
1905	858	187	4	3	..	1,052
1906	964	210	6	3	1	1,183
1907	892	194	7	3	1	1,096
1908	721	157	7	3	1	888
1909	941	205	4	3	1	1,153
1910	926	202	5	3	1	1,136
1911	901	197	7	3	1	1,108
1912	999	218	4	3	1	1,224
1913	1,071	234	4	3	1	1,312
1914	800	175	2	3	1	980
1915	798	174	1	4	1	976
1916	882	192	2	4	1	1,080
1917	856	187	9	4	1	1,056
1918	916	200	12	4	1	1,132
1919	1,325	289	15	4	1	1,633
1920	1,887	310	22	5	1	2,224
1921	1,382	297	33	8	1	1,720
1922	1,647	409	31	4	1	2,092
1923	2,393	385	38	7	1	2,824
1924	2,407	423	33	10	1	2,874
1925	2,393	556	60	13	1	3,023
1926	2,726	361	42	14	1	3,144
1927	2,634	398	49	14	1	3,096
1928	2,753	438	53	12	1	3,257
1929	2,704	439	64	17	1	3,225
1930	2,371	432	88	17	1	2,910
1931	1,579	309	42	14	1	1,945
1932	728	169	23	12	1	932
1933	602	130	20	10	1	762
1934	771	134	14	10	1	928
1935	861	160	13	9	1	1,043
1936	1,185	234	18	9	1	1,447
1937	1,482	294	20	9	1	1,806

[1] Less than $500,000.

TABLE 28: PERCENTAGE DISTRIBUTION OF REALIZED INCOME FROM CONSTRUCTION, BY KIND, 1899–1937

Year	Salaries and Wages	Entrepreneurial Income	Dividends	Interest	Net Rents and Royalties
1899	81.1	17.7	0.9	0.3	..
1900	81.0	17.7	1.0	0.3	..
1901	81.3	17.7	0.8	0.3	..
1902	81.3	17.8	0.7	0.2	..
1903	81.2	17.7	0.8	0.2	..
1904	81.4	17.7	0.5	0.3	..
1905	81.6	17.8	0.4	0.3	..
1906	81.5	17.8	0.5	0.3	..
1907	81.4	17.7	0.6	0.3	..
1908	81.2	17.7	0.8	0.3	..
1909	81.6	17.8	0.3	0.3	1
1910	81.5	17.8	0.4	0.3	1
1911	81.3	17.8	0.6	0.3	1
1912	81.6	17.8	0.3	0.2	1
1913	81.6	17.8	0.3	0.2	1
1914	81.6	17.9	0.2	0.3	1
1915	81.8	17.8	1	0.4	1
1916	81.7	17.8	0.2	0.4	1
1917	81.1	17.7	0.9	0.4	1
1918	80.9	17.7	1.1	0.4	1
1919	81.1	17.7	0.9	0.2	1
1920	84.8	13.9	1.0	0.2	1
1921	80.3	17.3	1.9	0.5	1
1922	78.7	19.6	1.5	0.2	1
1923	84.7	13.6	1.3	0.2	1
1924	83.8	14.7	1.1	0.3	1
1925	79.2	18.4	2.0	0.4	1
1926	86.7	11.5	1.3	0.4	1
1927	85.1	12.9	1.6	0.5	1
1928	84.5	13.4	1.6	0.4	1
1929	83.8	13.6	2.0	0.5	1
1930	81.5	14.8	3.0	0.6	1
1931	81.2	15.9	2.2	0.7	0.1
1932	78.1	18.1	2.5	1.3	1
1933	79.0	17.1	2.6	1.3	1
1934	83.1	14.4	1.5	1.1	1
1935	82.6	15.3	1.2	0.9	1
1936	81.9	16.2	1.2	0.6	0.1
1937	82.1	16.3	1.1	0.5	0.1

[1] Less than 0.05%.

TABLE 29: REALIZED INCOME FROM TRANSPORTATION, BY KIND, 1899–1937

Millions of Dollars

Year	Salaries and Wages	Entrepreneurial Income	Dividends	Interest	Net Rents and Royalties	Total, All Types
1899	967	72	123	306	..	1,468
1900	1,033	73	145	308	..	1,559
1901	1,095	73	156	320	..	1,644
1902	1,163	70	170	330	..	1,733
1903	1,257	74	201	341	..	1,873
1904	1,331	81	211	357	..	1,980
1905	1,402	87	229	374	..	2,092
1906	1,543	89	277	386	..	2,295
1907	1,614	86	293	410	..	2,403
1908	1,559	82	297	447	..	2,385
1909	1,616	80	323	474	1	2,494
1910	1,753	79	368	486	1	2,687
1911	1,824	78	360	498	1	2,761
1912	1,948	82	357	516	1	2,904
1913	2,039	86	379	534	1	3,039
1914	2,016	95	383	526	1	3,021
1915	2,078	111	359	571	1	3,120
1916	2,372	143	374	576	1	3,466
1917	2,834	186	369	577	1	3,967
1918	3,961	218	327	564	−3	5,067
1919	4,531	261	317	576	−3	5,682
1920	5,821	271	271	601	1	6,964
1921	4,625	274	237	625	1	5,762
1922	4,430	288	299	649	2	5,668
1923	4,906	318	303	668	2	6,197
1924	4,798	341	315	685	2	6,141
1925	4,859	364	365	683	2	6,273
1926	5,013	382	375	663	2	6,435
1927	4,938	386	473	653	2	6,452
1928	4,857	393	430	653	2	6,335
1929	4,968	410	502	644	2	6,525
1930	4,495	383	498	667	1	6,046
1931	3,797	352	342	654	1	5,146
1932	2,913	316	137	656	1	4,022
1933	2,719	309	117	586	1	3,733
1934	2,950	353	188	565	1	4,056
1935	3,215	392	191	554	1	4,353
1936	3,600	441	209	507	1	4,757
1937	3,889	459	225	418	1	4,991

[1] Less than $500,000.

TABLE 30: PERCENTAGE DISTRIBUTION OF REALIZED INCOME FROM TRANSPORTATION, BY KIND, 1899–1937

Year	Salaries and Wages	Entrepreneurial Income	Dividends	Interest	Net Rents and Royalties
1899	65.9	4.9	8.4	20.8	..
1900	66.3	4.7	9.3	19.8	..
1901	66.6	4.4	9.5	19.5	..
1902	67.1	4.0	9.8	19.0	..
1903	67.1	4.0	10.7	18.2	..
1904	67.2	4.1	10.7	18.0	..
1905	67.0	4.2	10.9	17.9	..
1906	67.2	3.9	12.1	16.8	..
1907	67.2	3.4	12.2	17.1	..
1908	65.4	3.4	12.5	18.7	..
1909	64.8	3.2	13.0	19.0	1
1910	65.2	2.9	13.7	18.1	1
1911	66.1	2.8	13.0	18.0	1
1912	67.1	2.8	12.3	17.8	1
1913	67.1	2.8	12.5	17.6	1
1914	66.7	3.1	12.7	17.4	1
1915	66.6	3.6	11.5	18.3	1
1916	68.4	4.1	10.8	16.6	1
1917	71.4	4.7	9.3	14.5	1
1918	78.2	4.3	6.5	11.1	2
1919	79.7	4.6	5.6	10.1	2
1920	83.6	3.9	3.9	8.6	1
1921	80.3	4.8	4.1	10.8	1
1922	78.2	5.1	5.3	11.5	1
1923	79.2	5.1	4.9	10.8	1
1924	78.1	5.6	5.1	11.2	1
1925	77.5	5.8	5.8	10.9	1
1926	77.9	5.9	5.8	10.3	1
1927	76.5	6.0	7.3	10.1	1
1928	76.7	6.2	6.8	10.3	1
1929	76.1	6.3	7.7	9.9	1
1930	74.3	6.3	8.2	11.0	1
1931	73.8	6.8	6.6	12.7	1
1932	72.4	7.9	3.4	16.3	1
1933	72.8	8.3	3.1	15.7	1
1934	72.7	8.7	4.6	13.9	1
1935	73.9	9.0	4.4	12.7	1
1936	75.7	9.3	4.4	10.7	1
1937	77.9	9.2	5.5	8.4	1

[1] Less than 0.05%.

[2] Negative.

TABLE 31: REALIZED INCOME FROM COMMUNICATION, BY KIND, 1899-1937

Millions of Dollars

Year	Salaries and Wages	Dividends	Interest	Net Rents and Royalties	Total, All Types
1899	39	16	5	..	60
1900	46	16	5	..	67
1901	53	18	5	..	76
1902	59	21	7	..	87
1903	62	25	8	..	95
1904	66	27	8	..	101
1905	82	27	9	..	118
1906	96	27	13	..	136
1907	94	29	18	..	141
1908	92	26	21	..	139
1909	100	36	17	1	154
1910	111	38	16	1	166
1911	127	39	17	1	184
1912	139	43	19	1	202
1913	153	44	22	2	221
1914	155	45	25	2	227
1915	151	48	25	2	226
1916	181	51	27	2	261
1917	214	57	28	3	302
1918	249	59	31	4	343
1919	309	59	35	4	407
1920	407	59	40	4	510
1921	405	67	44	4	520
1922	429	80	35	5	549
1923	474	93	39	5	611
1924	508	106	40	5	659
1925	531	118	50	6	705
1926	571	129	50	6	756
1927	590	144	51	6	791
1928	629	150	45	7	831
1929	707	168	44	7	926
1930	715	202	39	9	966
1931	640	217	39	7	903
1932	534	192	53	6	785
1933	460	191	56	5	712
1934	483	190	56	5	734
1935	504	193	55	5	757
1936	605	183	55	5	848
1937	702	182	54	5	943

TABLE 32: PERCENTAGE DISTRIBUTION OF REALIZED INCOME FROM COMMUNICATION, BY KIND, 1899–1937

Year	Salaries and Wages	Dividends	Interest	Net Rents and Royalties
1899	65.0	26.7	8.3	..
1900	68.7	23.9	7.5	..
1901	69.7	23.7	6.6	..
1902	67.8	24.1	8.0	..
1903	65.3	26.3	8.4	..
1904	65.3	26.7	7.9	..
1905	69.5	22.9	7.6	..
1906	70.6	19.9	9.6	..
1907	66.7	20.6	12.8	..
1908	66.2	18.7	15.1	..
1909	64.9	23.4	11.0	0.6
1910	66.9	22.9	9.6	0.6
1911	69.0	21.2	9.2	0.5
1912	68.8	21.3	9.4	0.5
1913	69.2	19.9	10.0	0.9
1914	68.3	19.8	11.0	0.9
1915	66.8	21.2	11.1	0.9
1916	69.3	19.5	10.3	0.8
1917	70.9	18.9	9.3	1.0
1918	72.6	17.2	9.0	1.2
1919	75.9	14.5	8.6	1.0
1920	79.8	11.6	7.8	0.8
1921	77.9	12.9	8.5	0.8
1922	78.1	14.6	6.4	0.9
1923	77.6	15.2	6.4	0.8
1924	77.1	16.1	6.1	0.8
1925	75.3	16.7	7.1	0.9
1926	75.5	17.1	6.6	0.8
1927	74.6	18.2	6.4	0.8
1928	75.7	18.1	5.4	0.8
1929	76.3	18.1	4.8	0.8
1930	74.0	20.9	4.0	0.9
1931	70.9	24.0	4.3	0.8
1932	68.0	24.5	6.8	0.8
1933	64.6	26.8	7.9	0.7
1934	65.8	25.9	7.6	0.7
1935	66.6	25.5	7.3	0.7
1936	71.3	21.6	6.5	0.6
1937	74.4	19.3	5.7	0.5

TABLE 33: REALIZED INCOME FROM TRADE, BY KIND, 1899–1937

Millions of Dollars

Year	Salaries and Wages	Entrepreneurial Income	Dividends	Interest	Net Rents and Royalties	Total, All Types
1899	1,638	612	55	5	268	2,578
1900	1,741	631	67	5	276	2,720
1901	1,848	650	70	5	285	2,858
1902	2,034	679	81	7	297	3,098
1903	2,161	710	82	8	311	3,272
1904	2,252	729	72	8	319	3,380
1905	2,527	752	75	9	329	3,692
1906	2,802	776	88	13	340	4,019
1907	2,873	821	97	18	359	4,168
1908	2,587	828	96	21	362	3,894
1909	2,956	859	102	17	376	4,310
1910	3,088	876	132	16	384	4,496
1911	3,126	870	154	17	381	4,548
1912	3,050	829	164	19	363	4,425
1913	3,446	950	247	22	416	5,081
1914	3,767	1,014	258	25	444	5,508
1915	3,893	1,028	280	25	451	5,677
1916	4,283	1,115	307	27	488	6,220
1917	4,780	1,248	375	28	547	6,978
1918	5,352	1,442	385	31	632	7,842
1919	6,289	1,705	401	35	747	9,177
1920	6,757	1,991	382	45	873	1,048
1921	5,781	1,646	320	43	721	8,511
1922	6,224	1,573	302	42	690	8,831
1923	7,019	1,608	369	24	705	9,725
1924	7,134	1,683	390	33	737	9,977
1925	7,536	1,666	440	33	730	10,405
1926	7,905	1,721	471	27	754	10,878
1927	7,716	1,714	495	33	751	10,709
1928	7,831	1,737	499	46	761	10,874
1929	8,200	1,823	566	60	798	11,446
1930	7,798	1,697	497	68	569	10,628
1931	6,776	1,543	386	64	358	9,126
1932	5,248	1,287	214	55	188	6,992
1933	4,625	1,122	179	49	158	6,132
1934	5,281	1,144	202	43	183	6,853
1935	5,685	1,154	207	35	227	7,309
1936	6,050	1,144	248	31	231	7,704
1937	6,673	1,176	296	31	238	8,414

TABLE 34: PERCENTAGE DISTRIBUTION OF REALIZED INCOME FROM TRADE, BY KIND, 1899–1937

Year	Salaries and Wages	Entrepreneurial Income	Dividends	Interest	Net Rents and Royalties
1899	63.5	23.7	2.1	0.2	10.4
1900	64.0	23.2	2.5	0.2	10.1
1901	64.7	22.7	2.4	0.2	10.0
1902	65.7	21.9	2.6	0.2	9.6
1903	66.0	21.7	2.5	0.2	9.5
1904	66.6	21.6	2.1	0.2	9.4
1905	68.4	20.4	2.0	0.2	8.9
1906	69.7	19.3	2.2	0.3	8.5
1907	68.9	19.7	2.3	0.4	8.6
1908	66.4	21.3	2.5	0.5	9.3
1909	68.6	19.9	2.4	0.4	8.7
1910	68.7	19.5	2.9	0.4	8.5
1911	68.7	19.1	3.4	0.4	8.4
1912	68.9	18.7	3.7	0.4	8.2
1913	67.8	18.7	4.9	0.4	8.2
1914	68.4	18.4	4.7	0.5	8.1
1915	68.6	18.1	4.9	0.4	7.9
1916	68.9	17.9	4.9	0.4	7.8
1917	68.5	17.9	5.4	0.4	7.8
1918	68.2	18.4	4.9	0.4	8.1
1919	68.5	18.6	4.4	0.4	8.1
1920	67.2	19.8	3.8	0.4	8.7
1921	67.9	19.3	3.8	0.5	8.5
1922	70.5	17.8	3.4	0.5	7.8
1923	72.2	16.5	3.8	0.2	7.2
1924	71.5	16.9	3.9	0.3	7.4
1925	72.4	16.0	4.2	0.3	7.0
1926	72.7	15.8	4.3	0.2	6.9
1927	72.1	16.0	4.6	0.3	7.0
1928	72.0	16.0	4.6	0.4	7.0
1929	71.6	15.9	4.9	0.5	7.0
1930	73.4	16.0	4.7	0.6	5.4
1931	74.2	16.9	4.2	0.7	3.9
1932	75.1	18.4	3.1	0.8	2.7
1933	75.4	18.3	2.9	0.8	2.6
1934	77.1	16.7	2.9	0.6	2.7
1935	77.8	15.8	2.8	0.5	3.1
1936	78.5	14.8	3.2	0.4	3.0
1937	79.3	14.0	3.5	0.4	2.8

TABLE 35: REALIZED INCOME FROM SERVICE INDUSTRIES, BY KIND, 1899–1937

Millions of Dollars

Year	Salaries and Wages	Entrepreneurial Income	Dividends	Interest	Net Rents and Royalties	Total, All Types
1899	1,160	587	9	1	−12	1,745
1900	1,179	596	11	1	−13	1,774
1901	1,186	600	12	1	−13	1,786
1902	1,208	611	13	1	−13	1,820
1903	1,240	627	14	1	−13	1,869
1904	1,264	640	12	1	−13	1,904
1905	1,287	651	13	2	−14	1,939
1906	1,308	662	15	2	−14	1,973
1907	1,368	692	16	3	−15	2,064
1908	1,400	708	16	4	−15	2,113
1909	1,688	854	17	3	−18	2,544
1910	1,693	857	22	3	−18	2,557
1911	1,661	840	26	5	−18	2,514
1912	1,564	791	27	6	−17	2,371
1913	1,769	895	41	6	−19	2,692
1914	1,860	941	43	8	−20	2,832
1915	1,860	941	47	9	−20	2,837
1916	1,990	1,007	51	12	−21	3,039
1917	2,195	1,110	62	14	−24	3,357
1918	2,507	1,269	64	17	−27	3,830
1919	2,928	1,481	67	20	−31	4,465
1920	3,575	1,809	64	26	−38	5,436
1921	3,570	1,806	53	31	−38	5,422
1922	3,532	1,787	50	35	−38	5,366
1923	3,888	1,967	70	46	−42	5,929
1924	4,238	2,144	73	59	−46	6,468
1925	4,421	2,237	94	73	−48	6,777
1926	4,891	2,474	108	88	−53	7,508
1927	4,928	2,493	110	122	−53	7,600
1928	5,155	2,608	102	141	−55	7,951
1929	5,392	2,728	120	196	−58	8,378
1930	4,977	2,639	119	211	−57	7,889
1931	4,198	2,477	79	180	−45	6,889
1932	3,233	2,025	56	125	−31	5,409
1933	2,930	1,877	34	72	−22	4,893
1934	3,279	2,044	42	64	−25	5,404
1035	3,619	2,286	80	62	−30	6,016
1936	3,910	2,613	110	55	−30	6,658
1937	4,229	2,761	125	49	−34	7,130

TABLE 36: PERCENTAGE DISTRIBUTION OF REALIZED INCOME FROM SERVICE INDUSTRIES, BY KIND, 1899–1937

Year	Salaries and Wages	Entrepreneurial Income	Dividends	Interest	Net Rents and Royalties
1899	66.5	33.6	0.5	0.1	−0.7
1900	66.5	33.6	0.6	0.1	−0.7
1901	66.4	33.6	0.7	0.1	−0.7
1902	66.4	33.6	0.7	0.1	−0.7
1903	66.3	33.5	0.7	0.1	−0.7
1904	66.4	33.6	0.6	0.1	−0.7
1905	66.4	33.6	0.7	0.1	−0.7
1906	66.3	33.6	0.8	0.1	−0.7
1907	66.3	33.5	0.8	0.1	−0.7
1908	66.3	33.5	0.8	0.2	−0.7
1909	66.4	33.6	0.7	0.1	−0.7
1910	66.2	33.5	0.9	0.1	−0.7
1911	66.1	33.4	1.0	0.2	−0.7
1912	66.0	33.4	1.1	0.3	−0.7
1913	65.7	33.2	1.5	0.2	−0.7
1914	65.7	33.2	1.5	0.3	−0.7
1915	65.6	33.2	1.7	0.3	−0.7
1916	65.5	33.1	1.7	0.4	−0.7
1917	65.4	33.1	1.8	0.4	−0.7
1918	65.5	33.1	1.7	0.4	−0.7
1919	65.6	33.2	1.5	0.4	−0.7
1920	65.8	33.3	1.2	0.5	−0.7
1921	65.8	33.3	1.0	0.6	−0.7
1922	65.8	33.3	0.9	0.7	−0.7
1923	65.6	33.2	1.2	0.8	−0.7
1924	65.5	33.1	1.1	0.9	−0.7
1925	65.2	33.2	1.4	1.1	−0.7
1926	65.1	33.0	1.4	1.2	−0.7
1927	64.8	32.8	1.4	1.6	−0.7
1928	64.8	32.8	1.3	1.8	−0.7
1929	64.4	32.6	1.4	2.3	−0.7
1930	63.1	33.5	1.5	2.7	−0.7
1931	60.9	36.0	1.1	2.6	−0.7
1932	59.8	37.4	1.0	2.3	−0.6
1933	59.9	38.4	0.7	1.5	−0.4
1934	60.7	37.8	0.8	1.2	−0.5
1935	60.2	38.2	1.3	1.0	−0.5
1936	58.7	39.2	1.7	0.8	−0.5
1937	59.3	38.7	1.8	0.7	−0.5

TABLE 37: REALIZED INCOME FROM FINANCE, BY KIND, 1899–1937

Millions of Dollars

Year	Salaries and Wages	Dividends	Interest	Net Rents and Royalties	Total, All Types
1899	202	89	47	−142	196
1900	239	91	51	−148	233
1901	290	100	53	−153	290
1902	347	130	56	−161	372
1903	393	121	62	−172	404
1904	438	144	64	−177	469
1905	454	139	66	−185	474
1906	428	170	72	−196	474
1907	389	176	80	−212	433
1908	412	192	81	−216	469
1909	462	190	80	−240	492
1910	497	210	89	−252	544
1911	539	224	93	−260	596
1912	582	229	99	−253	657
1913	622	229	108	−273	686
1914	630	224	110	−282	682
1915	675	218	113	−289	717
1916	764	229	117	−318	792
1917	840	243	132	−365	850
1918	963	253	145	−409	952
1919	1,267	270	159	−463	1,233
1920	1,507	292	193	−504	1,488
1921	1,558	309	199	−441	1,625
1922	1,567	329	190	−422	1,664
1923	1,740	363	216	−441	1,878
1924	1,903	385	227	−453	2,062
1925	2,010	487	245	−470	2,272
1926	2,192	466	272	−476	2,454
1927	2,354	459	290	−488	2,615
1928	2,519	568	312	−499	2,900
1929	2,696	711	317	−526	3,198
1930	2,503	578	397	−515	2,963
1931	2,215	492	418	−406	2,719
1932	1,896	308	276	−276	2,204
1933	1,718	165	150	−195	1,838
1934	1,807	191	31	−242	1,787
1935	1,898	207	−125	−288	1,692
1936	1,990	227	−293	−327	1,597
1937	2,135	248	−347	−362	1,674

TABLE 38: MISCELLANEOUS REALIZED INCOME, BY KIND, 1899–1937

Millions of Dollars

Year	Salaries and Wages	Entrepreneurial Income	Dividends	Interest	Net Rents and Royalties	Total, All Types
1899	467	326	151	75	−6	1,013
1900	497	341	169	76	−6	1,077
1901	536	355	187	81	−7	1,152
1902	584	375	207	86	−7	1,245
1903	629	396	208	90	−8	1,315
1904	640	411	197	95	−8	1,335
1905	704	428	212	101	−8	1,437
1906	763	446	259	108	−9	1,567
1907	798	476	287	115	−9	1,667
1908	720	484	268	121	−9	1,584
1909	830	506	283	127	−11	1,735
1910	886	509	342	130	−11	1,856
1911	896	499	315	135	−11	1,834
1912	937	468	318	139	−11	1,851
1913	1,017	530	295	145	−12	1,975
1914	995	559	229	145	−12	1,916
1915	1,033	559	221	155	−13	1,955
1916	1,222	598	640	158	−14	2,604
1917	1,444	662	715	161	−16	2,966
1918	1,753	756	637	163	−18	3,291
1919	2,026	882	506	170	−20	3,564
1920	2,430	1,067	184	178	−22	3,837
1921	1,886	1,055	284	187	−19	3,393
1922	1,946	1,037	− 46	193	−18	3,112
1923	2,319	1,130	−102	201	−19	3,529
1924	2,298	1,224	45	203	−20	3,750
1925	2,379	1,269	21	208	−21	3,856
1926	2,534	1,395	141	224	−21	4,273
1927	2,515	1,396	227	242	−21	4,359
1928	2,562	1,454	218	258	−22	4,470
1929	2,692	1,510	258	268	−23	4,706
1930	2,503	1,398	209	281	−20	4,371
1931	2,132	1,244	66	253	−11	3,684
1932	1,688	967	44	262	− 9	2,952
1933	1,608	905	− 13	251	− 7	2,744
1934	1,723	1,007	31	243	− 8	2,996
1935	1,843	1,069	82	242	−10	3,226
1936	2,091	1,222	91	235	− 7	3,632
1937	2,057	1,231	101	229	−10	3,608

TABLE 39: PERCENTAGE DISTRIBUTION OF MISCELLANEOUS REALIZED INCOME, BY KIND, 1899–1937

Year	Salaries and Wages	Entrepreneurial Income	Dividends	Interest	Net Rents and Royalties
1899	46.1	32.2	14.9	7.4	−0.6
1900	46.1	31.7	15.7	7.1	−0.6
1901	46.5	30.8	16.2	7.0	−0.6
1902	46.9	30.1	16.6	6.9	−0.6
1903	47.8	30.1	15.8	6.8	−0.6
1904	47.9	30.8	14.8	7.1	−0.6
1905	49.0	29.8	14.8	7.0	−0.6
1906	48.7	28.5	16.5	6.9	−0.6
1907	47.9	28.6	17.2	6.9	−0.5
1908	45.5	30.6	16.9	7.6	−0.6
1909	47.8	29.2	16.3	7.3	−0.6
1910	47.7	27.4	18.4	7.0	−0.6
1911	48.9	27.2	17.2	7.4	−0.6
1912	50.6	25.3	17.2	7.5	−0.6
1913	51.5	26.8	14.9	7.3	−0.6
1914	51.9	29.2	12.0	7.6	−0.6
1915	52.8	28.6	11.3	7.9	−0.7
1916	46.9	23.0	24.6	6.1	−0.5
1917	48.7	22.3	24.1	5.4	−0.5
1918	53.3	23.0	19.4	5.0	−0.5
1919	56.8	24.7	14.2	4.8	−0.6
1920	63.3	27.8	4.8	4.6	−0.6
1921	55.6	31.1	8.4	5.5	−0.6
1922	62.5	33.3	1	6.2	−0.6
1923	65.7	32.0	1	5.7	−0.5
1924	61.3	32.6	1.2	5.4	−0.5
1925	61.7	32.9	0.5	5.4	−0.5
1926	59.3	32.6	3.3	5.2	−0.5
1927	57.7	32.0	5.2	5.6	−0.5
1928	57.3	32.5	4.9	5.8	−0.5
1929	57.2	32.1	5.5	5.7	−0.5
1930	57.3	32.0	4.8	6.4	−0.5
1931	57.9	33.8	1.8	6.9	−0.3
1932	57.2	32.8	1.5	8.9	−0.3
1933	58.6	33.0	1	9.1	−0.3
1934	57.5	33.6	1.0	8.1	−0.3
1935	57.1	33.1	2.5	7.5	−0.3
1936	57.6	33.0	2.5	6.5	−0.3
1937	57.0	34.1	2.8	6.3	−0.3

¹ Negative.

CHAPTER IV

GOVERNMENT AS A SOURCE OF INCOME

GOVERNMENT activities that are rearranged and ex-
panded to meet emergency conditions tend to persist
at a higher level and to represent a permanent change in the
national economy, as may be seen by studying the long-term
trend of the national income and the government's increasing
importance as a source of income.

A comparison of the total realized income drived from private enterprise sources and from governmental sources is
presented in Table 40. A tremendous increase in the importance of government as a source of income during the past
century and a third is indicated. At the beginning of the
nineteenth century, only 1% of total national income was
derived from governmental sources, but by 1937 the proportion had increased to more than 16%. It reached 20% in
1936, as a result of the large soldiers' bonus payment in that
year. While the income from private enterprise sources as
shown by an index (base: 1929 = 100) increased from 1 in
1799 to 80 in 1937, the rise in income from governmental
sources in this period was from 0.1 to 163.

The importance of government as a direct source of the
incomes of individuals increased as much in the six years
from 1930 to 1936 as it had in the preceding 130 years.

Prior to the depressions commencing in the fall of 1929,
the principal gains in the importance of government as a
source of income have occurred in times of war. In the in-
terim periods, income derived from government has kept
pace, approximately, with that from private sources. After
an increase in importance from 1% to just under 2% in the
disturbed period from 1799 to 1819, there occurred no sig-

TABLE 40: REALIZED INCOME FROM GOVERNMENT, BY KIND, 1799–1937

Year	Realized Income from Government Million $	Percentage of Total Realized National Income	Production Income from Government[1] Million $	Other Income from Government[2] Million $	Percentage of Total Realized Income from Government	
					Production Income	Other Income
1799	6	0.9	6	..	100.0	..
1809	11	1.2	11	..	100.0	..
1819	17	1.9	15	2	3	3
1829	21	2.2	20	1	3	3
1839	39	2.4	37	2	3	3
1849	58	2.4	57	1	3	3
1859	101	2.3	100	1	99.0	1.0
1869	290	4.2	271	19	93.4	6.6
1879	322	4.5	284	38	88.2	11.8
1889	558	5.2	486	72	87.1	12.9
1899	1,005	6.5	910	95	90.5	9.5
1900	1,052	6.5	957	95	91.0	9.0
1901	1,052	6.1	956	96	90.9	9.1
1902	1,036	5.6	941	95	90.8	9.2
1903	1,091	5.5	996	95	91.3	9.7
1904	1,125	5.6	1,028	97	91.4	8.6
1905	1,155	5.4	1,058	97	91.6	8.4
1906	1,175	5.0	1,079	96	91.8	8.2
1907	1,234	5.0	1,139	95	92.3	7.7
1908	1,332	5.6	1,227	105	92.1	7.9
1909	1,398	5.3	1,286	112	92.0	8.0
1910	1,484	5.2	1,373	111	92.5	7.5
1911	1,557	5.5	1,446	111	92.9	7.1
1912	1,647	5.6	1,529	118	92.8	8.2
1913	1,752	5.5	1,627	125	92.9	7.1
1914	1,870	6.0	1,747	123	93.4	6.6
1915	1,964	6.0	1,843	121	93.8	6.2
1916	2,070	5.3	1,948	122	94.1	5.9
1917	2,700	5.8	2,569	131	95.1	4.9
1918	5,630	9.9	5,348	282	95.0	5.0
1919	5,410	8.6	5,060	350	93.5	6.5
1920	5,017	7.3	4,588	429	91.4	8.6
1921	5,307	9.3	4,819	488	90.8	9.2
1922	5,409	9.5	4,876	533	90.1	9.9
1923	5,572	8.5	5,091	481	91.4	8.6
1924	5,680	8.5	5,158	522	90.8	9.2
1925	5,902	8.4	5,414	488	91.7	8.3
1926	6,340	8.6	5,806	534	91.6	8.4
1927	6,580	8.9	6,019	561	91.5	8.5
1928	6,613	8.7	6,031	582	91.2	8.8
1929	6,819	8.6	6,197	622	90.9	9.1
1930	7,093	9.8	6,395	698	90.2	9.8
1931	7,317	12.1	6,438	879	88.0	12.0
1932	7,420	15.9	6,365	1,055	85.8	14.2
1933	7,785	17.4	6,063	1,723	77.9	22.1
1934	9,337	18.1	6,354	2,983	68.1	31.9
1935	10,135	18.0	6,744	3,392	66.5	33.5
1936	12,870	19.7	7,187	5,683	55.8	44.2
1937	11,566	16.7	7,993	3,573	69.1	30.9

[1] Salaries and wages of regular government employees and interest on government bonds.

[2] Pensions, compensation for injuries, relief and other government payments to individuals.

[3] Not significant owing to rounding of "other income" figures.

nificant change until the Civil War. During this period cash pensions to soldiers were insignificant, veterans of the War of 1812 and others being rewarded primarily with grants of government land. In the Civil War decade, from 1859 to 1869, the share of income supplied by government increased from 2.3% to 4.2%. After some further increase in the next thirty years, related in part to the increasing importance of pensions (which rose from $1 million in 1859 to $95 million in 1899) and the occurrence of the Spanish-American War, the government proportion showed only small fluctuations. The next major gain of government as a source of income occurred in the World War, the proportion jumping to 9.9% of the total realized national income.

The advent of the economic depressions in the latter part of 1929 brought about a further increase in the importance of government as a source of income. From 1930 to 1932 the share of government increased from 10% to 16%. This came about as a result of the drastic decline in income from private enterprise sources rather than through an increase in income from government, as the latter increased only from $7.1 billion to $7.4 billion in this time. However, as income from private sources increased after 1933, the importance of government as an income source was maintained at this high level, owing to the rapid increase in government expenditures. By 1936 and 1937, therefore, government sources, which had accounted for only $6 million, or only about 1% of the incomes of individuals at the beginning of the nineteenth century, were responsible for more than $11 billion of income, or nearly one-fifth of the total from all sources. (See Chart 9.)

Production income, or income derived from regular current government operations in the form of salaries and wages and interest on government bonds, segregated from other realized income from this source, is shown in the same table. Up to 1929 the other income consisted primarily of pensions, with a very minor amount of compensation for injuries. Notable are the increases in pensions after each war since the Civil War, and the tremendous increase in the importance of other income items after 1929.

CHART 9: REALIZED INCOME FROM GOVERNMENT AS A PERCENTAGE OF TOTAL REALIZED NATIONAL INCOME, 1799–1937

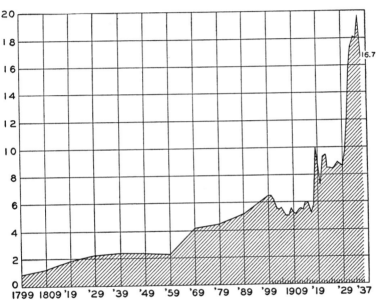

PRODUCTION INCOME FROM GOVERNMENT

Table 41 shows the segregation of salaries and wages from the interest component of government production income since 1899. The proportion of income derived from each of these sources remained fairly constant from 1899 until the World War, just under 90% being received in the form of salaries and wages.

Following the demobilization of emergency employees after the war and consequent upon the tremendous increase of gov-

TABLE 41: REALIZED PRODUCTION INCOME FROM GOVERNMENT, BY KIND, 1899–1937

Millions of Dollars

Year	Salaries and Wages	Interest	Total, All Types	Percentage Distribution	
				Salaries and Wages	Interest
1899	802	108	910	88.1	11.9
1900	847	110	957	88.5	11.5
1901	852	104	956	89.1	10.9
1902	838	103	941	89.1	10.9
1903	893	103	996	89.7	10.3
1904	920	108	1,028	89.5	10.5
1905	941	117	1,058	88.9	11.1
1906	953	126	1,079	88.3	11.7
1907	1,004	135	1,139	88.1	11.9
1908	1,086	141	1,227	88.5	11.5
1909	1,136	150	1,286	88.3	11.7
1910	1,214	159	1,373	88.4	11.6
1911	1,279	167	1,446	88.5	11.5
1912	1,352	177	1,529	88.4	11.6
1913	1,440	187	1,627	88.5	11.5
1914	1,533	214	1,747	87.8	12.2
1915	1,602	241	1,843	86.9	13.1
1916	1,685	263	1,948	86.5	13.5
1917	2,280	289	2,569	88.8	11.2
1918	4,874	474	5,348	91.1	8.9
1919	4,150	910	5,060	82.0	18.0
1920	3,254	1,334	4,588	70.9	29.1
1921	3,467	1,352	4,819	71.9	28.1
1922	3,490	1,386	4,876	71.6	28.4
1923	3,605	1,486	5,091	70.8	29.2
1924	3,748	1,410	5,158	72.7	27.3
1925	4,011	1,403	5,414	74.1	25.9
1926	4,394	1,412	5,806	75.7	24.3
1927	4,616	1,403	6,019	76.7	23.3
1928	4,630	1,401	6,031	76.8	23.2
1929	4,778	1,419	6,197	77.1	22.9
1930	4,946	1,449	6,395	77.3	22.7
1931	5,000	1,438	6,438	77.7	22.3
1932	4,855	1,510	6,365	76.3	23.7
1933	4,463	1,600	6,063	73.6	26.4
1934	4,655	1,708	6,354[1]	73.3	26.9
1935	5,104	1,660	6,744[1]	75.7	24.6
1936	5,450	1,757	7,187[1]	75.8	24.4
1937	6,155	1,850	7,993[1]	77.0	23.1

[1] Dividends received by the Reconstruction Finance Corporation on preferred stock of private corporations included as negative amounts: in 1933, less than $500,000; in 1934, $9,000,000; in 1935, $21,000,000; in 1936, $20,000,000; in 1937, $12,000,000. Dividends received by the Reconstruction Finance Corporation represent a deduction item of −0.1% in 1934 and −0.3% in 1935 and in 1936.

Billions of Dollars

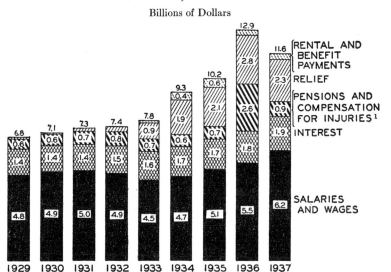

Percentage Distribution

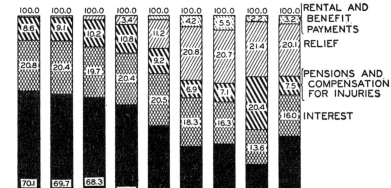

[1] Includes soldiers' bonus in 1936 and 1937.

91

ernment indebtedness, the proportion changed radically. From 1920 through 1923, just over 70% was received in salaries and wages, the interest portion having jumped from about 11% to just under 30%. The latter declined later as the war debt was being paid off, but never got below about double the prewar level. A remarkable feature is the failure of the interest proportion to rise permanently in recent years when government has been borrowing heavily to support an attempt to create purchasing power. Government and private developments which made private investment unattractive, as well as government intervention to control interest rates, have brought a great increase in government debt without sharply increasing interest payments.

OTHER INCOME FROM GOVERNMENT

The component items of other realized income from government are shown in Table 42. Prior to 1929 the pensions of regular government employees and war veterans, which account for almost all of the item, "pensions and compensation for injuries," constituted the whole of these other income sources. A great rise in pensions after the Civil War and after the World War is indicated.

After 1929 other government payments directly to individuals, exclusive of regular employees and bondholders, eclipsed the importance of pensions. The Federal Government, particularly, entered the field of national income on an entirely new basis. Not only was money distributed for the relief of distress, but a definite large-scale effort was undertaken to increase the national income by unprecedented cash disbursements of all kinds. Those going directly to individuals are included here under the heading "other income from government."

As is indicated in Chapter V, inclusion or exclusion of a specific government disbursement of cash to individuals — other than salaries and wages to regular employees and in-

TABLE 42: OTHER TYPES OF REALIZED INCOME FROM GOVERNMENT,
1799-1937

Year	Pensions and Compensation for Injuries	Year	Pensions and Compensation for Injuries	Year	Pensions and Compensation for Injuries	Year	Pensions and Compensation for Injuries
			Millions of Dollars				
1809[1]	. .[1]	1900	95	1910	111	1920	429
1819	2	1901	96	1911	111	1921	488
1829	1	1902	95	1912	118	1922	533
1839	2	1903	95	1913	125	1923	481
1849	1	1904	97	1914	123	1924	522
1859	1	1905	97	1915	121	1925	488
1869	19	1906	96	1916	122	1926	534
1879	38	1907	95	1917	131	1927	561
1889	72	1908	105	1918	282	1928	582
1899	95	1909	112	1919	350	. .	. .

Year	Pensions and Compensation for Injuries	Rental and Benefit Payments	Work Relief	Direct Relief	Total, Other Realized Income
		Millions of Dollars			
1929	589	. .	. .	33	622
1930	644	. .	2	52	698
1931	748	. .	23	108	879
1932	804	. .	52	199	1,055
1933	719	131	456	417	1,723
1934	648	395	1,243	697	2,983
1935	726	558	1,273	834	3,392
1936	2,636[2]	287	2,320	440	5,683
1937	874	367	1,782	550	3,573
		Percentage Distribution			
1929	94.7	. .	. .	5.3	100.0
1930	92.3	. .	0.3	7.4	100.0
1931	85.1	. .	2.6	12.3	100.0
1932	76.2	. .	4.9	18.9	100.0
1933	41.7	7.6	26.5	24.2	100.0
1934	21.7	13.2	41.7	23.4	100.0
1935	21.4	16.5	37.5	24.6	100.0
1936	46.4	5.1	40.8	7.7	100.0
1937	24.5	10.3	49.9	15.4	100.0

[1] Also negligible in 1799.

[2] Includes 1,873 million dollars paid in connection with the Soldiers' Bonus in 1936 and 26 million dollars paid in 1937.

terest to holders of government bonds—can be about equally well rationalized from the economic standpoint. The course pursued here has been to include all the items of importance: pensions, compensation for injuries, work relief, direct relief, rental and benefit payments to farmers and the soldiers' bonus distribution of 1936. Items excluded are very small and there is no adequate record of them available; they include such receipts of individuals from government as special rewards for services rendered and fees paid persons, such as consultants and jurors, not on the regular payroll.

The other income items mentioned above, which are included in the total income derived from government sources, reached a peak of between $5 billion and $6 billion in 1936. Recently, relief, both work and direct, has accounted for more than half of the total, while rental and benefit payments to farmers have assumed an important position. In 1936 the soldiers' bonus of nearly $2 billion was paid, temporarily increasing the importance of the pension item.

CHAPTER V

MISCELLANEOUS REALIZED INCOME ITEMS

BEYOND the income derived directly from the recognized private industries and occupations, there are other items of income which form a definite part of the total national income from private sources; and there are still other items of a borderline nature for which either the inclusion or exclusion can be equally rationalized from the economic standpoint. In addition to the salaries and wages, entrepreneurial income, dividends, interest, and net rents and royalties, which have been included in the private production income totals discussed in Chapters II and III, the following items are included as "miscellaneous" in the national income total from private sources presented in this study: net rent from farm and non-farm homes, interest from mortgages on owned homes, pensions, compensation for injuries and work and direct relief from private sources.[1]

There are a great many additional items of an income nature which are, for practical or theoretical reasons, troublesome to the income estimator. Taking the usual position that no income has been created unless a useful productive service has been performed in connection with the transfer of purchasing power, it is still possible to justify equally well either inclusion or exclusion of debatable items. In the last analysis, the individual estimator's general judgment, in view of the purpose for which the estimates are to be used, must be relied upon to make wise decisions. As regards an item like government rental and benefit payments to farmers, for example, a case can be made not only for exclusion, but for actual deduction of the item from the income total, on the ground that the purchasing power does not arise from production but from a deliberate *decrease* in production. The

---

[1] For miscellaneous income items of government origin, see Chapter IV.

CHART 11: MISCELLANEOUS REALIZED INCOME ITEMS OF PRIVATE ORIGIN, 1799–1937

Millions of Dollars

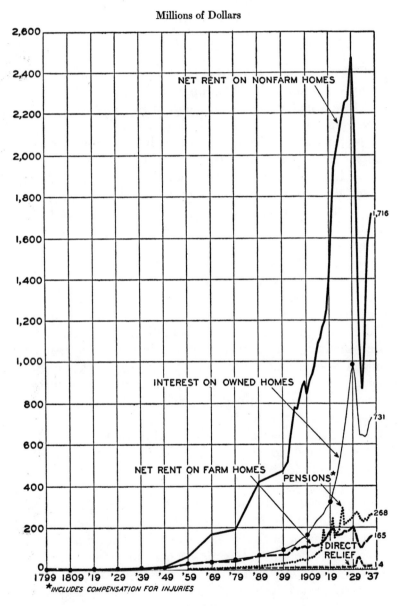

*INCLUDES COMPENSATION FOR INJURIES

position taken here, however, is that it is obviously the judgment of society as a whole that farmers are performing a useful public service by curtailing production, or society would not be paying therefor; and the item is neither deducted nor omitted, but included. (See Chapter IV.)

Another type of difficulty occurs where items are clearly of an income nature, but source data for estimating them are scanty or lacking. Again the judgment of the estimator must be relied upon to strike a balance between the needs for accuracy of estimates and for completeness of coverage.

Either because in the judgment of the estimator the items are not clearly of an income nature, or because basic data are lacking, the following items of an income nature have been excluded from consideration in these estimates:

Income from odd jobs
Expense accounts of employees
Bonuses and similar supplementary income, and, in part, commissions received by employees
Pensions paid informally
Income from unorganized charity and similar gifts
Income from roomers and boarders, including tourists
Income from urban gardens, poultry, etc.
Illegal income
Profits or losses from the sale of assets or property
Changes in the value of assets or property held
Changes in the value of commodity inventories
Business savings or losses
Uncompensated services of members of families
Imputed income, or hypothetical income from ownership of durable goods by individuals using them

The total realized income of private origin, with a breakdown between the private production income portion and the miscellaneous income items, is shown in Table 43.

The miscellaneous items, which were insignificant at the

TABLE 43: REALIZED NATIONAL INCOME OF PRIVATE ORIGIN, 1799–1937

Year	Private Production Income	Miscellaneous Income of Private Origin	Total Realized Income of Private Origin	Per Cent of Total Realized Income Production Income	Per Cent of Total Realized Income Miscellaneous Income
		Millions of Dollars			
1799	668	3	671	99.6	0.4
1809	901	3	904	99.7	0.3
1819	855	4	859	99.5	0.5
1829	947	7	954	99.3	0.7
1839	1,577	15	1,592	99.1	0.9
1849	2,326	36	2,362	98.5	1.5
1859	4,098	112	4,210	97.3	2.7
1869	6,288	249	6,537	96.2	3.8
1879	6,617	288	6,905	95.8	4.2
1889	9,578	565	10,143	94.4	5.6
1899	13,836	663	14,499	95.4	4.6
1900	14,550	696	15,246	95.4	4.6
1901	15,537	721	16,258	95.6	4.4
1902	16,705	843	17,548	95.2	4.8
1903	17,691	953	18,644	94.9	5.1
1904	18,059	1,046	19,105	94.5	5.5
1905	19,363	1,050	20,413	94.9	5.1
1906	21,008	1,122	22,130	94.9	5.1
1907	22,112	1,197	23,309	94.9	5.1
1908	21,049	1,217	22,266	94.5	5.5
1909	24,033	1,164	25,197	95.4	4.6
1910	25,569	1,256	26,825	95.3	4.7
1911	25,385	1,309	26,694	95.1	4.9
1912	26,559	1,367	27,926	95.1	4.9
1913	28,391	1,462	29,853	95.1	4.9
1914	27,954	1,539	29,493	94.8	5.2
1915	29,114	1,588	30,702	94.8	5.2
1916	35,032	1,748	36,780	95.2	4.8
1917	42,014	1,778	43,792	95.9	4.1
1918	49,520	1,897	51,417	96.3	3.7
1919	55,539	2,078	57,617	96.4	3.6
1920	60,995	2,495	63,490	96.1	3.9
1921	48,763	2,691	51,454	94.8	5.2
1922	49,036	2,791	51,827	94.6	5.4
1923	57,213	2,954	60,167	95.1	4.9
1924	58,178	3,223	61,401	94.8	5.2
1925	60,949	3,284	64,233	94.9	5.1
1926	63,857	3,427	67,284	94.9	5.1
1927	63,942	3,546	67,488	94.7	5.3
1928	65,653	3,779	69,432	94.6	5.4
1929	68,872	3,940	72,812	94.6	5.4
1930	61,968	3,464	65,432	94.7	5.3
1931	50,066	2,857	52,923	94.6	5.4
1932	37,132	2,176	39,308	94.5	5.5
1933	35,074	1,885	36,959	94.9	5.1
1934	40,205	2,087	42,292	95.1	4.9
1935	44,037	2,204	46,241	95.2	4.8
1936	49,852	2,716	52,568	94.8	5.2
1937	54,959	2,894	57,853	95.0	5.0

TABLE 44: PERCENTAGE DISTRIBUTION OF MISCELLANEOUS INCOME ITEMS OF PRIVATE ORIGIN, 1799–1937

Year	Net Rent on Non-Farm Homes	Net Rent on Farm Homes	Interest on Owned Homes	Pensions and Compensation for Injuries	Direct Relief	Work Relief
1799	. .	66.7	33.3	. .	. .	. .
1809	33.3	33.3	33.3	. .	. .	. .
1819	25.0	25.0	50.0	. .	. .	. .
1829	42.9	14.3	42.9	. .	. .	. .
1839	40.0	20.0	40.0	. .	. .	. .
1849	41.7	30.6	27.8	. .	. .	. .
1859	55.4	21.4	21.4	0.9	0.9	. .
1869	69.9	14.1	14.5	1.2	0.4	. .
1879	67.7	12.8	16.0	2.4	1.0	. .
1889	74.0	11.2	11.9	2.5	0.5	. .
1899	71.0	10.0	14.3	3.9	0.8	. .
1900	71.7	9.9	13.6	4.0	0.7	. .
1901	71.4	9.7	14.0	4.2	0.7	. .
1902	73.0	9.7	12.8	3.9	0.6	. .
1903	74.0	9.7	12.0	3.9	0.5	. .
1904	75.0	9.7	11.4	3.4	0.5	. .
1905	73.9	9.3	12.5	3.8	0.5	. .
1906	73.9	9.2	12.7	3.8	0.4	. .
1907	73.8	9.1	12.8	3.9	0.4	. .
1908	74.4	9.0	12.8	3.4	0.4	. .
1909	72.5	8.7	14.3	4.0	0.4	. .
1910	72.1	8.6	14.6	4.4	0.3	. .
1911	71.3	8.9	15.3	4.3	0.3	. .
1912	71.2	8.3	15.7	4.5	0.4	. .
1913	70.8	7.9	15.8	5.1	0.3	. .
1914	70.6	7.7	15.9	5.5	0.3	. .
1915	70.3	7.6	15.9	5.7	0.4	. .
1916	66.6	7.5	15.1	10.5	0.3	. .
1917	67.0	8.3	16.4	7.9	0.3	. .
1918	66.2	8.7	16.0	8.8	0.4	. .
1919	62.2	9.1	15.5	8.1	0.3	. .
1920	67.4	7.7	15.0	9.6	0.3	. .
1921	72.1	6.8	15.1	5.7	0.3	. .
1922	71.0	5.9	16.1	5.9	0.3	. .
1923	70.1	5.5	17.5	6.6	0.3	. .
1924	67.1	5.2	18.2	9.2	0.2	. .
1925	67.2	5.6	20.4	6.6	0.2	. .
1926	65.7	5.3	22.1	6.6	0.3	. .
1927	64.0	5.3	23.9	6.6	0.3	. .
1928	63.3	5.1	24.8	6.5	0.3	. .
1929	62.8	5.1	25.1	6.7	0.3	. .
1930	60.4	4.7	26.6	7.9	0.4	0.1
1931	57.9	4.3	26.8	9.2	1.2	0.5
1932	51.9	4.7	29.7	11.2	1.9	0.6
1933	46.5	5.6	34.1	12.3	1.1	0.4
1934	51.5	5.8	30.5	11.5	0.6	1
1935	52.9	6.2	29.4	10.8	0.6	1
1936	58.1	5.7	26.1	9.6	0.5	1
1937	59.3	5.7	25.3	9.3	0.4	1

[1] Less than 0.05%.

1929 = 100

Year	Net Rent on Non-Farm Homes	Net Rent on Farm Homes	Interest on Owned Homes	Pensions and Compensation for Injuries	Direct Relief	Total,[1] All Items
1799	..	1.0	0.1	..	..	0.1
1809	[2]	0.5	0.1	..	..	0.1
1819	[2]	0.5	0.2	..	..	0.1
1829	0.1	0.5	0.3	..	..	0.2
1839	0.2	1.5	0.6	..	..	0.4
1849	0.6	5.4	1.0	..	..	0.9
1859	2.5	11.9	2.4	0.4	10.0	2.8
1869	7.0	17.3	3.6	1.1	10.0	6.3
1879	7.9	18.3	4.7	2.7	30.0	7.3
1889	16.9	31.2	6.8	5.3	30.0	14.3
1899	19.0	32.7	9.6	9.8	50.0	16.8
1900	20.2	34.2	9.6	10.6	50.0	17.7
1901	20.8	34.7	10.2	11.4	50.0	18.3
1902	24.8	40.6	10.9	12.5	50.0	21.4
1903	28.5	45.5	11.5	14.0	50.0	24.2
1904	31.7	50.0	12.0	13.6	50.0	26.5
1905	31.3	48.5	13.3	15.2	50.0	26.6
1906	33.5	51.0	14.4	16.3	50.0	28.5
1907	35.7	54.0	15.5	17.8	50.0	30.4
1908	36.6	54.5	15.8	15.5	50.0	30.9
1909	34.1	50.0	16.9	17.8	50.0	29.5
1910	36.6	53.5	18.5	20.8	40.0	31.9
1911	37.7	57.4	20.2	21.2	40.0	33.2
1912	39.3	55.9	21.8	23.1	50.0	34.7
1913	41.8	57.4	23.4	28.4	50.0	37.1
1914	43.9	58.4	24.8	31.8	50.0	39.1
1915	45.1	59.9	25.6	34.5	60.0	40.3
1916	47.0	64.9	26.7	69.3	60.0	44.4
1917	48.1	73.3	29.6	53.4	60.0	45.1
1918	50.7	81.7	30.8	62.9	70.0	48.1
1919	56.2	93.6	32.6	63.6	70.0	52.7
1920	67.9	95.0	37.9	90.9	80.0	63.3
1921	78.4	90.6	41.1	58.3	70.0	68.3
1922	81.0	81.2	45.3	62.9	70.0	70.8
1923	83.7	80.7	52.2	73.9	80.0	75.0
1924	87.3	83.7	59.4	112.5	80.0	81.8
1925	89.1	90.6	67.9	81.8	80.0	83.4
1926	91.0	90.1	76.7	85.2	90.0	87.0
1927	91.6	93.1	85.7	88.6	90.0	90.0
1928	96.6	96.0	94.9	92.8	100.0	95.9
1929	100.0	100.0	100.0	100.0	100.0	100.0
1930	84.5	81.2	93.1	103.0	150.0	87.9
1931	66.8	60.9	77.6	99.6	350.0	72.5
1932	45.6	50.5	65.4	92.0	420.0	55.2
1933	35.4	52.5	65.1	87.9	210.0	47.8
1934	43.4	60.4	64.4	91.3	130.0	53.0
1935	47.1	67.8	65.6	90.5	130.0	55.9
1936	63.7	76.7	71.7	98.9	130.0	68.9
1937	69.3	81.7	74.0	101.5	130.0	73.5

[1] Includes "Work Relief" payments since 1930.
[2] Less than 0.05%.

beginning of the nineteenth century, reached a total of just under \$4 billion in 1929. They increased greatly in relative importance in the total realized income of private origin during the nineteenth century, rising from 0.3% in 1809 to 5.6% in 1889, and fluctuating later between 3.5% and 5.5%.

Net rent on farm and non-farm homes has accounted for between one-half and three-fourths of the total of these miscellaneous income items of private origin. Interest on owned homes has been next in importance, while the most rapidly rising item has been pensions and compensation for injuries.

Net International Transfers

There remains an adjusting income item, arising from international transfers of interest and dividends which cannot be allocated between private and government sources. Data are lacking prior to 1909, and the adjustment of the total realized income estimates by this item have been made only for subsequent years. On balance, as will be observed in Table 46, more interest and dividends have been sent abroad than have been received from foreign countries, making the item negative. This negative item was probably of greater relative weight in the total during the nineteenth century than since, and, were the quantities known, would have considerably reduced the estimates for the early years.

TABLE 46: NET INTERNATIONAL TRANSFERS OF DIVIDENDS
AND INTEREST, UNITED STATES, 1909–1936 [1]
Millions of Dollars

Year	Transfers	Year	Transfers	Year	Transfers
1909	−139	1919	− 82	1928	−141
1910	−143	1920	− 73	1929	−133
1911	−147	1921	− 72	1930	−127
1912	−151	1922	− 65	1931	− 37
1913	−155	1923	− 77	1932	− 20
1914	−150	1924	− 78	1933	− 31
1915	−133	1925	− 84	1934	− 69
1916	−111	1926	−101	1935	−122
1917	−116	1927	−102	1936	−192
1918	− 91				

[1] Adjustments for balance of international payments of dividends and interest.

APPENDIX

SOURCES AND METHODS

THE regular National Industrial Conference Board national income estimates for recent years have been basic to those presented herewith. The work of other previous investigators has also been fully utilized, and in this connection the studies of the dean of national income estimators, Dr. Willford I. King, who placed his worksheets and advice at our disposal, have been indispensable. Industry data from 1919 to 1929, prepared by Dr. Simon Kuznets, have also been extensively utilized as indicators of major trends in this period. The work of others that has been drawn upon in a minor way will be noticed in the details following. The principal items in all of these references have been checked back to original sources.

Special note should be made here of the fact that in many instances data shown in these estimates will be found not to check directly with the figures in some original sources, such as the Census of Manufactures. In recent years the classifications of some of the subdivisions of manufacturing have had to be transferred to other industries to make the industrial grouping consistent with that used in the Statistics of Income source data. In early years, as a result of intensive search, it was found that the census data that were officially known to understate the actual situation could be adjusted for the major known shortages, and this was done.

This description of sources and methods is presented in two sections, the first covering the annual estimates from 1899 to 1928 and the second relating to the Census years from 1799 to 1899. The outline of sources and methods used in preparing the estimates for 1929 and subsequent years is omitted since it has remained essentially unchanged from that explained in the sources and methods appendix of the Board's earlier work, "The National Income and Its Elements."[1]

[1] Robert F. Martin, "National Income and Its Elements," National Industrial Conference Board, New York, 1936, pp. 93 ff.

105

A. NATIONAL INCOME, ANNUAL, 1899–1928

1. Salaries and Wages

AGRICULTURE

The 1929 estimate of salaries and wages in agriculture was projected to 1919 on the basis of Dr. Kuznets' estimates for this industry.[1]

The 1919 estimate was projected to 1909 on the basis of Dr. King's corresponding estimates.[2]

The 1909 estimate thus derived was projected to 1899 in the following manner: the number of farm laborers for 1909 and for 1899 were taken from the Census of Occupations, 1910 and 1900, and estimates for the other years were based on data on the volume of agricultural production.[3] Ratios, for 1899 and 1909, of the number of farm laborers to the volume of agricultural production were computed and interpolated for the other years. The ratios were then applied to the annual estimates of the volume of agricultural production, thus securing estimates of the number of farm laborers from 1899 to 1909. The product of the estimated number of farm laborers and average annual wages in agriculture, as estimated by Professor Douglas for the respective years,[4] was used as indicative of the trend from 1899 to 1909.

MINING AND QUARRYING

The 1929 estimate was projected to 1919 on the basis of Dr. Kuznets' estimates of salaries and wages.[5]

The 1919 estimate was projected to 1909 on the basis of Dr. King's estimates for the respective years.[6]

The 1909 estimate, thus obtained, was projected to 1899 on the

---

[1] Simon Kuznets, "Income Originating in Nine Basic Industries, 1919–1934." National Bureau of Economic Research, New York, Bulletin, May 4, 1936.

[2] Willford I. King, "National Income and its Purchasing Power," National Bureau of Economic Research, New York, 1930.

[3] Nourse and Associates, "America's Capacity to Produce," The Brookings Institution, Washington, D. C., 1934.

[4] Paul H. Douglas, "Real Wages in the United States, 1890–1926," Publication No. 9 of the Pollak Foundation for Economic Research, Newton, Massachusetts, 1930.

[5] Kuznets, *op. cit.*, Appendix, Table 1, p. 22.

[6] King, *op. cit.*, pp. 132, 138.

basis of the combined estimates for salaries and wages derived from the following sources:

Anthracite and Bituminous Coal Mining

Salaries and wages for 1902 and 1909 were taken from the Census of Mines and Quarries, 1902 and 1919.

In estimating the other years, the total labor force less the number of unemployed in coal-mining, as estimated by Professor Douglas,[1] was taken as to represent the number of employees from 1899 to 1909. Estimates of salaries and wages from 1899 to 1909 were then obtained as the product of the number of employees and average earnings in coal-mining, as estimated by Professor Douglas,[2] for each year. The estimates of salaries and wages thus derived were then adjusted to the census figures for total salaries and wages. Ratios of the census figures to these estimates were computed for 1902 and 1909 and interpolated for the other years. The 1902 ratio was assumed constant for the years prior to 1902. Final estimates of salaries and wages were arrived at by multiplying the ratios, thus secured, by the annual estimates derived from the product of the number of employees and average earnings.

Producing Gas and Oil Wells

Salaries and wages for 1902 and 1909 were taken from the Census of Mines and Quarries for 1919. Estimates for the other years were based on data on the value of petroleum production.[3] Ratios of salaries and wages (census) to the value of petroleum production were computed for 1902 and 1909 and interpolated for the other years. From 1899 to 1902, the 1902 ratio was assumed constant. Final estimates of salaries and wages were obtained by applying these ratios to the annual data on the value of petroleum production.

ELECTRIC LIGHT AND POWER AND GAS

Total salaries and wages were derived from 1899 to 1929 by using the sum of estimates made for: (1) electric light and power, and manufactured gas; and (2) natural gas.

[1] Douglas, *op. cit.*, p. 457.

[2] *Ibid.*, Table 147.

[3] United States Department of the Interior, Bureau of Mines, "Minerals Yearbook," 1937, p. 1009.

Electric Light and Power and Manufactured Gas

The 1929 estimate of salaries and wages for this industrial group was projected to 1919 on the basis of Dr. Kuznets' estimates for the corresponding years.[1]

The 1919 estimate thus derived was projected to 1909 on the basis of Dr. King's estimates of salaries and wages.[2]

The 1909 estimate was then projected to 1899 on the basis of the trend of salaries and wages estimated for (a) electric light and power and (b) manufactured gas, obtained as follows:

(a) Electric Light and Power

Total salaries, wages and the number of employees are given in the 1932 Census of Electrical Industries, Central Electric Light and Power Stations. The number of employees for 1902, 1907, and 1912 were taken from the census and interpolated for the other years. The average of the difference between the census figures for 1907 and those for 1902 was used to project the 1902 census figures for the number of employees to 1899. Estimates of salaries and wages were then obtained by multiplying the estimated number of employees by annual average earnings in the gas and electricity industry, as estimated by Professor Douglas.[3] These estimates were then adjusted to the census figures for total salaries and wages. Ratios of salaries and wages (census) to the estimates thus obtained were computed for the years 1902, 1907 and 1912, and interpolated for the years in between. The 1902 ratio was used for the years from 1899 to 1902. Total salaries and wages were finally obtained by applying the ratios thus secured to the annual estimates derived from the product of the number of employees and average annual earnings as described above.

(b) Manufactured Gas

Total salaries, wages and the number of employees are given in the Census of Manufactures. The number of employees for 1899, 1904, and 1909 were taken from the census, and estimates for the other years were based on data on the volume of sales of manufactured gas from 1901 to 1909, as reported by the American Gas Association.[4] Ratios of the number of employees to the sales of manu-

---

[1] Kuznets, *op. cit.*, Appendix, Table 1, p. 22.

[2] King, *op. cit.*, pp. 132, 138.   [3] Douglas, *op. cit.*, p. 334.

[4] "Annual Statistics of the Manufactured Gas Industry in the United States," Statistical Bulletin, No. 9, October, 1931, p. 32.

factured gas for 1904 and 1909 were computed and interpolated for the other years. The ratio for 1904 was assumed constant for the years from 1899 to 1904. Estimates of the number of employees from 1899 to 1909 were obtained by multiplying the ratios by the annual estimates of the sales of manufactured gas. The estimated numbers of employees were then multiplied by annual average earnings in the gas and electricity industry, as estimated by Professor Douglas.[1] The estimates thus derived were adjusted to the census figures for total salaries and wages. Ratios of total salaries and wages (census) to the estimates of salaries and wages were computed for 1899, 1904 and 1909 and interpolated or extrapolated for all other years. Total salaries and wages were derived by applying the ratios thus secured to the annual estimates of salaries and wages from 1899 to 1909.

Natural Gas

Total salaries and wages were projected from 1899 to 1929 on the basis of the trend of the volume of natural gas purchased during the period. The estimates of the volume of natural gas purchased were derived as follows: the volume of natural gas produced and consumed from 1906 to 1919, as reported in the "Minerals Yearbook, 1937," p. 1062, was projected to 1899 on the basis of the value of natural gas produced and consumed from 1899 to 1906 as given in "Mineral Resources, 1915," Part II, p. 933. Finally, the volume of natural gas purchased from 1919 to 1929, as estimated by the American Gas Association,[2] was projected to 1899 on the basis of the volume of natural gas produced and consumed annually from 1899 to 1919 as derived by the above methods.

MANUFACTURING

The 1929 estimate of salaries and wages was projected to 1919 on the basis of Dr. Kuznets' estimates of salaries and wages in manufacturing for these years.[3]

The 1919 estimate thus derived was projected to 1909 on the basis of Dr. King's estimates for the respective years.[4]

Separate estimates for salaries and wages were made for the years from 1899 to 1909, and the 1909 estimate of salaries and

---

[1] Douglas, *op. cit.*, p. 334.   [2] "Annual Statistics," *op. cit.*, p. 32.
[3] Kuznets, *op. cit.*, Appendix, Table 1, p. 22.
[4] King, *op. cit.*, pp. 132, 138.

wages, obtained above, was projected to 1899 on the basis of the trend of these combined estimates.

Wages paid in manufacturing for 1899, 1904 and 1909 were taken from the Census of Manufactures, and were adjusted to correspond with the national income classification of manufacturing as an industrial group by deducting wages paid in the shipbuilding, railroad repair and manufactured gas industries. In estimating the other years, the number of wage earners[1] was multiplied by average earnings, as estimated by Professor Douglas,[2] for each year. Ratios of wages (census) to the estimates thus secured were computed for 1899, 1904 and 1909 and interpolated for the other years. Final estimates of wages from 1899 to 1909 were obtained by applying these ratios to the annual estimates of wages derived from the product of the number of wage earners and average earnings.

Total salaries and the number of salaried employees (excluding shipbuilding, railroad repair and manufactured gas) for 1899, 1904 and 1909 in this industry were likewise derived from the Census of Manufactures. Ratios of the number of salaried employees to the number of wage earners (census) were computed for 1899, 1904 and 1909 and interpolated for the other years. Estimates of the number of salaried employees from 1899 to 1909 were then obtained by applying the resulting ratios to the annual estimates of the number of wage earners. The numbers of salaried employees thus derived were multiplied by annual average earnings of salaried employees in manufacturing, as estimated by Professor Douglas.[3] These estimates likewise were adjusted to the figures for total salaries based on census data. Ratios of salaries (census) to the estimates of salaries were computed for 1899, 1904 and 1909 and interpolated for the other years. Total salaries from 1899 to 1909 were then obtained by multiplying these ratios by the annual estimates of salaries, derived for each year as the product of the number of employees and the average salary.

CONSTRUCTION

The 1929 estimate of salaries and wages was projected to 1919 on the basis of Dr. Kuznets' estimates for contract construction for the corresponding years.[4]

[1] National Industrial Conference Board, *Conference Board Bulletin*, Feb. 25, 1937, p. 34.

[2] Douglas, *op. cit.*, p. 246.   [3] *Ibid.*, p. 361.

[4] Kuznets, *op. cit.*, Appendix, Table 1, p. 22.

The 1919 estimate was then projected to 1909 on the basis of Dr. King's estimates for this industry.[1]

The 1909 estimate of salaries and wages thus obtained was projected to 1899 on the basis of a trend of salaries and wages for these years. This trend was computed by the following methods:

Estimates of the number of employees in the building trades from 1909 to 1899 were reached by deducting the number of unemployed from the total labor force for this industry, as estimated by Professor Douglas[2] for the respective years. The number of employees for each year was then multiplied by an annual average of full-time weekly earnings, as estimated by Professor Douglas.[3] The estimates of total earnings from 1899 to 1909 thus obtained were converted to index numbers using 1909 as the base.

Next, the number of employees, derived as shown above, was multiplied by average earnings of wage-earners in manufacturing, as estimated by Professor Douglas,[4] for each year from 1899 to 1909. The second estimates of total annual earnings thus secured from 1899 to 1909 were likewise converted to index numbers on a 1909 base.

An arithmetical average of the indexes of the two separate estimates of total earnings from 1899 to 1909 was used to obtain final estimates of salaries and wages in this industry.

TRANSPORTATION

Salaries and wages were estimated separately for three groups of transportation enterprises: (1) Steam railroads, Pullman and express; (2) street railways, pipe lines and water transportation; and (3) motor, truck and air transportation. The 1929 estimate for total transportation was then projected to 1899 on the basis of the trend of the combined estimates made for the selected groups.

Steam Railroads, Pullman and Express

The 1929 estimate of salaries and wages was projected to 1919 on the basis of Dr. Kuznets' estimates for this group of transportation.[5]

The 1919 estimate was projected to 1909 on the basis of Dr. King's separate estimates for railroads, Pullman and express, combined.[6]

---

[1] King, *op. cit.*, pp. 132, 138.   [2] Douglas, *op. cit.*, p. 455.   [3] *Ibid.*, p. 137.
[4] *Ibid.*, p. 246.   [5] Kuznets, *op. cit.*, Appendix, Table 1, p. 22.
[6] King, *op. cit.*, pp. 132–138.

The 1909 estimate was then projected to 1899 on the basis of the trend of total compensation paid by all operating carriers, including switching and terminal companies,[1] as reported in the "Statistics of Railways."

Street Railways, Pipe Lines and Water Transportation

The 1929 estimate was projected to 1919 on the basis of Dr. Kuznets' estimates for this group.[2]

The 1919 estimate was projected to 1909 on the basis of Dr. King's separate estimates for street railways and water transportation, combined.

The 1909 estimate thus obtained was projected to 1899 on the trend of the sums of estimates made for water transportation and street railways.

Water Transportation

Salary and wage estimates for 1900 and 1910 are taken from Dr. King.[3] Estimates for the other years are based on annual data on the tonnage of sailing and steam vessels of the merchant marine of the United States, employed in foreign and coastwide trade and in the fisheries.[4] Ratios of Dr. King's estimate of salaries and wages in water transportation to the total tonnage of steam and sailing vessels were computed for 1900 and 1910 and interpolated for the other years. The 1900 ratio was assumed constant for 1899. The ratios were applied to the annual data on the gross tonnage, securing a probable trend of salaries and wages in water transportation from 1899 to 1909.

Street Railways

Salaries and wages in the group are taken directly from the 1932 Census of Electrical Industries for 1902, 1907 and 1912. In estimating the other years, the annual number of employees in this industry was multiplied by average annual earnings as estimated by Professor Douglas,[5] for each year from 1899 to 1909. Ratios of

---

[1] Interstate Commerce Commission, "Statistics of Railways," 1900, p. 466, cited in "Statistical Abstract of the United States, 1936," p. 375.

[2] Kuznets, *op. cit.*, Appendix, Table 1, p. 23.

[3] Willford I. King, "The Wealth and Income of the People of the United States," National Bureau of Economic Research, New York, 1919, p. 260.

[4] "Statistical Abstract of the United States, 1911," p. 302.

[5] Douglas, *op. cit.*, pp. 334, 440.

salaries and wages (census) to these estimates were computed for 1902, 1907 and 1912 and interpolated for the other years. The 1902 ratio was assumed for the years from 1899 to 1902. Final estimates of salaries and wages were arrived at by multiplying the ratios thus secured by the annual estimates of salaries and wages obtained from the product mentioned above of the number of employees multiplied by average annual earnings.

Motor, Truck and Air Transportation

Salaries and wages for 1909, 1919 and 1929 were derived directly from census data. For each of these years the number of chauffeurs and drivers, as reported in the 1930 Census of Occupations, was multiplied by average wages in manufacturing, obtained from data in the 1929 Census of Manufactures. In estimating totals for the other years, the combined total of salaries and wages and entrepreneurial income for 1929 was projected to 1909 on the basis of data on the total number of cars registered annually from 1909 to 1929, as reported by the National Automobile Chamber of Commerce and the Bureau of Public Roads.[1] Final estimates of salaries and wages were made on the basis of the ratios of salaries and wages (based on census data) to the estimates of total salaries and wages and entrepreneurial income obtained as described above.

As in the period 1909–1929, salaries and wages for 1899 and 1909 were estimated by the use of census data and by following the same procedure. Ratios of salaries and wages (based on census data) to final estimated salaries and wages in street railways (1899–1909, as previously described) were computed for 1899 and 1909 and interpolated for the other years. Final estimates of salaries and wages in motor, truck and air transportation from 1899 to 1909 were obtained by multiplying the ratios thus secured by the annual estimates of total salaries and wages in street railways.

COMMUNICATION

The 1929 estimate was projected to 1909 on the basis of Dr. Kuznets' estimates of salaries and wages.[2]

The 1919 estimate was projected to 1909 on the basis of Dr. King's separate estimates for telephones and telegraphs, combined for the respective years.[3]

[1] "Statistical Abstract of the United States, 1933," p. 334.

[2] Kuznets, op. cit., Appendix, Table 1, p. 23.

[3] "National Income and its Purchasing Power," op. cit., pp. 132, 138.

The 1909 estimate thus derived was projected to 1899 on the basis of the trend of combined salaries and wages, estimated separately for telephones and telegraphs as follows:

Telephones

Salaries and wages for 1902, 1907 and 1912 are taken directly from the 1932 Census of Electrical Industries. In estimating for the other years, the number of employees in each year from 1899 to 1909, as furnished by the American Telephone and Telegraph Company, was multiplied by Professor Douglas' estimates of average earnings in this industry from 1902 to 1909.[1] (Douglas' estimate of average wages in 1902 was projected to 1899 on the basis of his estimates of average annual earnings in gas and electricity.) The estimates thus obtained were then adjusted to the census figures. Ratios of salaries and wages (census) to the estimates of salaries and wages were computed for 1902, 1907 and 1912 and interpolated for the other years. The 1902 ratio was assumed constant for the years 1899–1902 inclusive. Final estimates of total salaries and wages were obtained by applying these ratios to the annual estimates of salaries and wages described above.

Telegraphs

The number of employees and total salaries and wages are obtained directly from the 1932 Census of Electrical Industries for 1902, 1907 and 1912. The number of messages sent, as reported annually by the Western Union Telegraph Company, was used to indicate the trend of employment. Annual estimates of the number of employees from 1899 to 1909 were obtained by applying this trend to the number of employees as given for 1902, 1907 and 1912 in the census. The estimated numbers of employees, thus derived, were multiplied by average annual earnings in the telegraph industry, as estimated by Professor Douglas.[2] The ratios of salaries and wages (census) to the estimates thus derived were computed for 1902, 1907 and 1912 and interpolated for the other years. The 1902 ratio was used for the years from 1899 to 1902. Final estimates of total salaries and wages were arrived at by applying the ratios thus obtained to the annual estimates of salaries and wages described above.

[1] Douglas, *op. cit.*, p. 334.   [2] *Idem.*

TRADE

The 1929 estimate was projected to 1919 on the basis of Dr. Kuznets' estimates of salaries and wages.[1]

The 1919 estimate was projected to 1909 on the basis of Dr. King's estimates of salaries and wages in the mercantile industry.[2]

The 1909 estimate was then projected to 1899 by means of an index of the trend of earnings estimated as follows:

The tons of revenue freight carried, as reported annually by the Interstate Commerce Commission,[3] and the composite index of agricultural, mineral and manufacturing production, as estimated by Dr. Nourse,[4] were converted to index numbers for the years 1899–1909 on a 1909 base. An arithmetical average was taken of the two series of index numbers for each year and the resulting series used to represent the trend of employment from 1899 to 1909.

For the same period, an arithmetical average was taken of average annual salaries and wages in manufacturing and steam railroads, as estimated by Professor Douglas,[5] and indexes computed on a 1909 base. From the indexes of average earnings thus derived, a trend of total payrolls was estimated from the product of the index of employment (obtained as described above) and the index of average wages.

FINANCE

The total salary and wage item in this industry is the sum of salaries and wages estimated separately for banking, insurance and real estate, from 1909 to 1929. Since there is a lack of adequate data on these separate items from 1899 to 1909, it was impossible to project the estimates separately. The combined estimate of salaries and wages in finance for 1909 was therefore projected to 1899 on the basis of other data indicating a probable trend for this period. The sources and methods used were as follows:

Banking

The 1929 estimate was projected to 1919 on the basis of Dr. Kuznets' estimates for this item.[6]

[1] Kuznets, *op. cit.*, Appendix, Table 1, p. 23.

[2] "National Income and its Purchasing Power," *op. cit.*, pp. 132, 138.

[3] "Statistical Abstract of the United States, 1911," p. 745.

[4] Nourse and Associates, *op. cit.*, p. 547.

[5] Douglas, *op. cit.*, Table 147.

[6] Simon Kuznets, "National Income and Capital Formation, 1919–1935." National Bureau of Economic Research, New York, 1937. p. 65.

The 1919 estimate was projected to 1909 on the basis of Dr. King's estimates for the group.[1]

Insurance

The 1929 estimate was projected to 1919 on the basis of Dr. Kuznets' corresponding estimates.[2]

The 1919 estimate was projected to 1909 on the basis of salaries and wages and agents' commissions in the field of life insurance, taken for the respective years from the "Life Insurance Yearbook," published by the Spectator Company.

Real Estate

The 1929 estimate was projected to 1919 on the basis of Dr. Kuznets' estimates of salaries and wages in real estate.[3]

The 1919 estimate was projected to 1909 by using an index of the trend of salaries and wages, computed as follows:

The number of real estate agents and officials, as reported in the Census of Occupations, was multiplied by an average salary in banking, as estimated by Dr. King,[4] for the years 1909 and 1919 respectively. The estimates thus secured for the census years were converted to index numbers on a 1919 base. Indexes of salaries and wages in banking and insurance from 1909 to 1919 were then adjusted to the index numbers of the estimates of salaries and wages in real estate for the census years. Final estimates of salaries and wages in real estate were based on the adjusted indexes thus derived.

The 1909 estimate of total salaries and wages in finance was projected to 1899 as follows: The number of persons gainfully occupied in banking, insurance and real estate, as reported in the Census of Occupations, was multiplied by the average salary in manufacturing and steam railroads combined, as estimated by Professor Douglas[5] for 1899 and 1909. The results were converted to index numbers on a 1909 base and used to represent total salaries and wages in finance for the census years 1899 and 1909. Index numbers of salaries and wages in the life insurance field from 1899 to 1909, computed from data in the Life Insurance Yearbooks, were adjusted to the indexes of total salaries and wages in finance for

---

[1] "National Income and its Purchasing Power," *op. cit.*, p. 138.
[2] "National Income and Capital Formation, 1919–1935," *op. cit.*, p. 65.
[3] *Idem.*
[4] "National Income and its Purchasing Power," *op. cit.*, p. 158.
[5] Douglas, *op. cit.*, Table 147.

the census years. Final estimates of salaries and wages in finance were made on the basis of the adjusted trend thus secured.

SERVICE

The 1929 estimate for total salaries and wages in all service industries combined was projected to 1899 on the basis of a trend of salaries and wages computed as follows:

The number of those gainfully occupied in personal, business, professional, recreation and amusement, domestic and miscellaneous services was taken from the Census of Occupations for each census year. Estimates for the other years were based on a straight-line interpolation between the figures for the census years. The separate annual estimates thus secured for the period from 1899 to 1929 were continued to obtain the total number of gainfully occupied in all service industries. From the estimates derived in this way, a trend of salaries and wages from 1899 to 1929 was obtained by multiplying the total number of gainfully occupied in Service in each year by an estimate of average annual earnings. For the period from 1909 to 1929, Dr. King's estimates of annual average earnings in the mercantile industry were used.[1] From 1899 to 1909 an average of Professor Douglas' estimates of average annual earnings for manufacturing and steam railroads, teachers and ministers was used.[2]

GOVERNMENT

The 1929 estimate of salaries and wages was projected to 1927 on the basis of the trend of the results obtained, by deducting government interest payments from Dr. Leven's estimates of realized income from government for the years 1927, 1928 and 1929.[3]

Total government interest payments for 1927, 1928 and 1929 included federal interest payments (obtained from the Annual Reports of the Secretary of the Treasury) and state and local interest payments, as published by the National Industrial Conference Board in its annual "Cost of Government" series.

The 1927 estimate of salaries and wages was projected to 1909

[1] "National Income and its Purchasing Power," op. cit., p. 146.

[2] Douglas, op. cit., Table 147.

[3] Maurice Leven and others, "America's Capacity to Consume," The Brookings Institution, Washington, D. C., 1934.

on the basis of Dr. King's estimates of salaries and wages in government for these years.[1]

The 1909 estimate was then projected to 1899 on the basis of a trend of salaries and wages obtained by combining the results of two methods of estimating.

The first method gave estimates of salaries and wages as indicated by the product of the total number of government employees and an average salary and wage payment for each year from 1899 to 1909.

The total number of government employees used for this purpose included: the active personnel in the United States Army, Navy, Marine Corps and National Guard, obtained from the Annual Reports of the War and Navy Departments; the total number of postal employees, obtained from the Annual Reports of the Postmaster General; other officials and inspectors of the United States, and state, county and city officials, inspectors and employees, estimated on the basis of data obtained from the Census of Occupations for 1900 and 1910.

The average figures for salary and wage payments used were obtained by taking arithmetical averages of Professor Douglas' estimate of average annual earnings for postal employees, government employees (executive department) and teachers for each year from 1899 to 1909.[2]

By the second method, salaries and wages for 1899 were estimated by applying the percentage change of Dr. King's estimates of salaries and wages in government from 1900 to 1910[3] to the 1909 estimate. Ratios of these figures for total salaries and wages to the estimates of salaries and wages obtained by the first method, were computed for 1899 and 1909 and interpolated for the other years.

The final trend of salaries and wages from 1899 to 1909 was estimated by applying the ratios derived from the second method to the annual estimates of salaries and wages as first obtained.

MISCELLANEOUS

The 1929 estimate of salaries and wages was projected to 1899 on the basis of the trend of all the foregoing industries combined.

---

[1] "National Income and its Purchasing Power," *op. cit.*, p. 138.

[2] Douglas, *op. cit.*, Table 147.

[3] "Wealth and Income," *op. cit.*, p. 260.

2. Entrepreneurial Income

AGRICULTURE

The 1929 estimate was projected to 1919 on the basis of Dr. Kuznets' estimates for withdrawals by farm operators.[1]

The 1919 estimate was projected to 1909 on the basis of Dr. King's estimates for income of entrepreneurs and of property in agriculture.[2]

The 1909 estimate was then projected to 1899 on the basis of the trend of the value of farm products, as estimated by the United States Department of Agriculture, adjusted by the ratio of farm income to the value of products for postwar years.

MINING AND QUARRYING

The 1929 estimate was projected to 1919 on the basis of Dr. Kuznets' estimates for withdrawals by entrepreneurs in this industry.[3]

The 1919 estimate thus derived was projected to 1899 on the basis of a trend of entrepreneurial income estimated as follows:

The numbers of mining operators for 1899, 1909 and 1919 were taken from the 1929 Census of Mines and Quarries, and estimated by interpolation for the other years. The number of entrepreneurs thus obtained was multiplied by an average wage in mining, estimated by Dr. King from 1909 to 1919.[4] The 1919 estimate of total entrepreneurial income in mining was then projected to 1909 on the basis of this trend. The 1909 estimate was projected to 1899 on the basis of the trend of the product of the number of entrepreneurs in each year and an average wage in mining, as estimated by Professor Douglas.[5]

MANUFACTURING

The 1929 estimate was projected to 1919 on the basis of Dr. Kuznets' estimates of withdrawals by entrepreneurs.[6]

The 1919 estimate was then projected to 1899 on the basis of indexes of the trend of entrepreneurial income computed as follows: Salaries and wages, the number of salaried employees and wage

---

[1] "Income in Nine Basic Industries," *op. cit.*, Appendix, Table 1, p. 22.

[2] "National Income and Its Purchasing Power," *op. cit.*, p. 306.

[3] "Income in Nine Basic Industries," *op. cit.*, Appendix, Table 1, p. 22.

[4] "National Income and Its Purchasing Power," *op. cit.*, p. 146.

[5] Douglas, *op. cit.*, Table 147.

[6] "Income in Nine Basic Industries," *op. cit.*, Appendix, Table 1, p. 22.

earners, and the number of proprietors and firm members were taken from the 1929 Census of Manufactures for the census years. An average salary and wage payment was computed for each census year on the basis of the data on salaries and wages and salaried employees and wage earners. Estimates of entrepreneurial income for the census years 1899, 1904, 1909, 1914 and 1919 were then obtained by multiplying the average salary and wage payments thus derived by the number of proprietors and firm members. The 1909, 1914 and 1919 estimates of entrepreneurial income were converted to index numbers on a 1919 base. Estimates of the trend of entrepreneurial income for the other years were made on the basis of the ratio of these index numbers to index numbers of Dr. King's annual estimates of salaries and wages in manufacturing from 1909 to 1919.[1] From 1899 to 1909 the same procedure was followed, using 1909 as the base year for the index numbers of the census estimates for 1899, 1904 and 1909, and estimating the other years on the basis of the ratios of these index numbers to the estimated salaries and wages in manufacturing from 1899 to 1909, obtained as described above under the section on salaries and wages.

CONSTRUCTION

The 1929 estimate of entrepreneurial income was projected to 1919 on the basis of Dr. Kuznets' estimates of withdrawals by entrepreneurs for the respective years.[2]

The 1919 estimate thus secured was projected to 1899 on the basis of the trend of the estimates of salaries and wages from 1919 to 1899 obtained as described under salaries and wages in the section on construction.

TRANSPORTATION

Entrepreneurial income in transportation is the sum of separate estimates made for two groups within this industry.

Street Railways, Pipe Lines and Water Transportation

The 1929 estimate of entrepreneurial income for this group was projected to 1919 on the basis of Dr. Kuznets' estimates of withdrawals by entrepreneurs.[3]

---

[1] "National Income and Its Purchasing Power," op. cit., pp. 132, 138.
[2] "Income in Nine Basic Industries," op. cit., Appendix, Table 1, p. 22.
[3] Idem.

The 1919 estimate of entrepreneurial income was then projected to 1899 on the basis of the trend of salaries and wages for these industries.

Motor, Truck and Air Transportation

The 1929 estimate was projected to 1899 on the basis of the trend of salaries and wages for this group.

TRADE

The 1929 estimate was projected to 1919 on the basis of Dr. Kuznets' estimates of entrepreneurial income in trade.[1]

The 1919 estimate thus obtained was projected to 1899 on the basis of the trend of entrepreneurial income, estimated for this period as follows: The numbers of wholesale and retail merchants and dealers were taken from the Census of Occupations for 1899, 1909 and 1919 and obtained for the other years by interpolation. The numbers of wholesale and retail merchants and dealers, thus secured, were multiplied by annual average earnings in trade for each year from 1899 to 1919. For the period from 1909 to 1919, Dr. King's estimates of average annual earnings in the mercantile industry were used.[2] From 1899 to 1909, arithmetical averages of Professor Douglas' estimates of average salaries and wages in manufacturing and in steam railroads were used.[3]

SERVICE

The 1929 estimate of entrepreneurial income was projected to 1899 on the basis of the trend of salaries and wages for this industry.

MISCELLANEOUS

The 1929 estimate was projected to 1899 on the basis of a trend of entrepreneurial income derived as the product of the estimated number of entrepreneurs, and the average compensation.

The number of entrepreneurs in fishing, brokerage, the miscellaneous professions and the various hand trades, was taken from the Census of Occupations for 1899, 1909, 1919 and 1929 and interpolated separately for the other years. The separate estimates were

---

[1] "Income in Nine Basic Industries," *op. cit.*, Appendix, Table 1, p. 22.

[2] "National Income and Its Purchasing Power," *op. cit.*, p. 146.

[3] Douglas, *op. cit.*, Table 147.

added to arrive at the total number of entrepreneurs for the miscellaneous group as a whole.

From 1909 to 1929, Dr. King's estimates of annual average earnings in the mercantile industry[1] were used for the average compensation in this industry. From 1899 to 1909, arithmetical averages of Professor Douglas' estimates of average salaries and wages in manufacturing and on steam railroads were used.[2]

3. Dividends

AGRICULTURE

The dividend data used for the estimates for 1922–1929 were obtained from the United States Treasury Department. The figures for cash dividends paid, published annually in the "Statistics of Income," were adjusted to eliminate dividends received by corporations from other domestic corporations, as given in the same report. The 1929 estimate of net dividends was then projected to 1922 on the basis of the results thus obtained.

The 1922 estimate of net dividends in agriculture was projected to 1899 on the basis of the trend of net dividends in mining and quarrying for these years.

MINING AND QUARRYING

The 1929 estimate of net dividends was projected to 1919 on the basis of Dr. Kuznets' estimates of dividends for this industry.[3]

The 1919 estimate was projected to 1909 on the basis of Dr. King's estimates of net dividends on preferred and common stock for mines, quarries, and oil wells combined.[4]

The 1909 estimate of net dividends thus derived was projected to 1899 on the basis of a sample of corporation reports tabulated from data obtained for the respective years from Moody's Manuals.

ELECTRIC LIGHT AND POWER AND GAS, AND MANUFACTURING

The sources and methods used in estimating net dividends for these industries were identical with those used for mining and quarrying.

[1] "National Income and Its Purchasing Power," *op. cit.*, p. 146.
[2] Douglas, *op. cit.*, Table 147.
[3] "Income in Nine Basic Industries," *op. cit.*, Appendix, Table 1, p. 22.
[4] "National Income and Its Purchasing Power," *op. cit.*, pp. 189, 191.

CONSTRUCTION

The 1929 estimate was projected to 1919 on the basis of Dr. Kuznets' estimates of dividends for the respective years.[1]

The 1919 estimate thus derived was projected to 1899 on the basis of a sample of corporation reports tabulated from data obtained for the respective years from Moody's Manuals.

TRANSPORTATION

The 1929 estimate of net dividends in this industry was projected to 1899 on the basis of the combined results from 1899 to 1929 of separate estimates made for the following groups:

Steam Railroads, Pullman and Express

The 1929 estimate was projected to 1919 on the basis of Dr. Kuznets' estimates of dividends for this group.[2]

The 1919 estimate was then projected to 1909 on the basis of Dr. King's estimates of net dividends on common and preferred stock for these industries combined.[3]

The 1909 estimate thus derived was projected to 1899 on the basis of data on dividends for the respective years obtained from the "Statistics of Railways," published annually by the Interstate Commerce Commission.

Street Railways, Pipe Lines and Water Transportation

The 1929 estimate of net dividends for this group was projected to 1919 on the basis of Dr. Kuznets' estimates of dividends.[4]

The 1919 estimate was then projected to 1909 on the basis of Dr. King's estimates of net dividends on common and preferred stock paid to individuals by street railway corporations.[5]

The 1909 estimate thus derived was projected to 1899 on the basis of a sample of corporation reports tabulated from data from Moody's Manuals on street railways and water transportation for the respective years.

[1] "Income in Nine Basic Industries," *op. cit.*, Appendix, Table 1, p. 22.

[2] *Idem.*

[3] "National Income and Its Purchasing Power," *op. cit.*, pp. 189, 191.

[4] Kuznets, *supra.*

[5] King, *supra.*

COMMUNICATION

Estimates of net dividend payments in this industry from 1909 to 1929 are derived from the same sources and by the same methods that have been described in the section on mining and quarrying for the respective years.

Estimates for the period from 1899 to 1909 were reached by projecting the 1909 estimate to 1899 on the basis of data on dividends obtained from the annual reports of the American Telephone and Telegraph Company and those of the Western Union Telegraph Company for the respective years.

TRADE

The 1929 estimate was projected to 1919 on the basis of Dr. Kuznets' estimates of dividends in trade.[1]

The 1919 estimate was projected to 1909 on the basis of a sample of corporation reports tabulated from data obtained for the respective years from Moody's Manuals.

The 1909 estimate of net dividends was then projected to 1899 on the basis of the trend of net dividends, estimated for manufacturing and transportation, combined for each year from 1899 to 1909.

FINANCE

Estimates of net dividends in finance from 1922 to 1929 were based on data obtained from the same source, and were reached by the same method, as described under agriculture for the corresponding period.

The 1922 estimate of net dividends was then projected to 1899 on the basis of the trend of dividends paid on common stock by the National Banks, as shown in the Annual Reports of the Comptroller of Currency for the respective years.

SERVICE AND MISCELLANEOUS

Estimates of net dividends for these industries from 1922 to 1929 were likewise based on data obtained from the annual "Statistics of Income" and were computed by the same method as described for agriculture in this period.[2]

---

[1] "Income in Nine Basic Industries," *op. cit.*, Appendix, Table 1, p. 23.

[2] "Statistics of Income," United States Treasury Department, Washington, D. C.

Estimated net dividends in the service industry for the other years were procured by projecting the 1922 estimate to 1909 on the basis of the trend of estimated net dividends obtained for trade for these years. The 1909 estimate, thus secured, was then projected to 1899 on the basis of the combined net dividends estimated separately for manufacturing and transportation for the respective years.

In the miscellaneous industry group, estimates of net dividends from 1899 to 1922 were obtained by projecting the 1922 estimate to 1899 on the basis of the trend of the sum of the estimates of the foregoing industries.

4. Interest

AGRICULTURE

The 1929 estimate was projected to 1919 on the basis of Dr. Kuznets' estimates of interest on mortgages for this industry.[1]

The 1919 estimate thus obtained was then projected to 1899 on the basis of estimates of the Conference Board's Research Staff,[2] by Leonard Kuvin, of interest charges on farm mortgages.

Mining and Quarrying, Electric Light and Power and Gas, Manufacturing, Transportation and Communication

The 1929 estimates of net interest for these industries were projected to 1919 on the basis of Dr. Kuznets' corresponding estimates of interest for these years.[3]

The 1919 estimates were projected to 1909 on the basis of Dr. King's estimates of net interest on funded debt for the corresponding industries.[4]

The estimates for these industries from 1899 to 1909, were procured by projecting the 1909 estimates, thus derived, to 1899 as follows: mining, manufacturing, and transportation were projected on the basis of Mr. Kuvin's annual estimates of interest charges on bonded debt and mortgages for the respective industries.[5] Electric light and power and gas and communication were projected on the basis of the results obtained when the annual

---

[1] "Income in Nine Basic Industries," *op. cit.*, Appendix, Table I, p. 22.

[2] Leonard Kuvin, "Private Long-Term Debt and Interest in the United States," National Industrial Conference Board, Inc., New York, September, 1936.

[3] Kuznets, *supra.*

[4] "National Income and Its Purchasing Power," *op. cit.*, p. 186.

[5] Kuvin, *op. cit.*, pp. 44, 46.

amounts of funded debt for the respective industries were multiplied by the interest rates on public utility funded debt as estimated by Mr. Kuvin.[1]

CONSTRUCTION

The 1929 estimate was projected to 1919 on the basis of Dr. Kuznets' estimates of interest for this industry.[2]

The 1919 estimate thus secured was projected to 1909 on the basis of the trend of the estimates of interest obtained for manufacturing in the respective years.

The 1909 estimate was then projected to 1899 on the basis of Mr. Kuvin's estimates of interest charges on industrial funded debt.[3]

TRADE

The 1929 estimate of net interest was projected to 1919 on the basis of Dr. Kuznets' estimates of interest in trade for these years.[4]

The 1919 estimate thus secured was projected to 1899 on the basis of the estimates of net interest obtained for communication for the corresponding period.

FINANCE

Estimates of net interest payments in finance were obtained by projecting the sum of estimates made for: (1) interest paid on savings deposits; and (2) interest paid on corporate debt and individual non-farm mortgages.

In estimating interest payments on savings deposits, estimates of the total amounts of savings deposits for all reporting banks were obtained from data in the Annual Reports of the Comptroller of Currency as follows:

From 1921 to 1929, the total amounts of savings deposits of all reporting banks were taken as shown.

From 1909 to 1921, the 1921 figure for total savings deposits was projected to 1909 on the basis of the amounts of savings deposits of mutual and stock savings banks combined for these years.

The 1909 estimate thus derived was projected to 1899 on the basis of the total amounts of savings deposits of all savings banks for the respective years.

---

[1] Kuvin, *op. cit.*, pp. 30, 50.

[2] "Income in Nine Basic Industries," *op. cit.*, Appendix, Table I, p. 22.

[3] Kuvin, *op. cit.*, p. 46.

[4] Kuznets, *supra*.

The total amounts of savings deposits from 1899 to 1929 were then multiplied by the percentage yield for each year of high grade corporate bonds.[1] By projecting the 1929 estimate of interest paid on savings deposits to 1899 on the basis of the results, the annual estimates of interest payments on savings deposits were reached.

Estimates of interest payments on corporate debt and individual non-farm mortgages were obtained by projecting the 1929 estimate to 1899 on the basis of the annual amounts of interest charges on total real estate mortgages as estimated by Mr. Kuvin.[2]

SERVICE

The 1929 estimate of net interest payments in the service industry was projected to 1909 on the basis of the results obtained by deducting interest charges on the long-term debt of manufacturing and mining from interest charges on industrial long-term debt for the respective years as estimated by Mr. Kuvin.[3]

The 1909 estimate was then projected to 1899 on the basis of the trend of estimated net interest payments in communication for the respective years.

GOVERNMENT

The 1929 estimate of net interest payments made by the government to individuals was projected to 1899 on the basis of total government interest payment figures, for the respective years, as compiled by Lewis H. Kimmel of the Conference Board's Research Staff.

MISCELLANEOUS

The 1929 estimate of net interest payments in the miscellaneous group was projected to 1899 on the basis of a trend of net interest payments derived for these years as follows: Dr. King's estimates of net interest payments on funded debt for "All Other Industries"[4] were taken for the years 1909 to 1925. The 1925 figure was projected to 1929, and the 1909 figure to 1899, on the basis of Mr. Kuvin's estimates of interest charges on total private long-term debt for the respective years.[5]

[1] "Standard Statistics Basebook," Vol. 80, No. 26, Sec. 5, p. B-110.
[2] Kuvin, *op. cit.*, p. 42.   [3] *Ibid.*, pp. 42, 46.
[4] "National Income and Its Purchasing Power," *op. cit.*, p. 186.
[5] Kuvin, *op. cit.*, p. 46.

5. Net Rents and Royalties

AGRICULTURE

The 1929 estimate of net rents and royalties in agriculture was projected to 1899 on the basis of estimates for these years derived from data indicating a probable trend.

The amounts of net rent paid by farmers to non-farmer landlords, as estimated by the United States Department of Agriculture,[1] were used for the years 1924–1929 inclusive. The 1924 figure was projected to 1909 on the basis of Dr. King's estimates of gross rent payments to non-farmer landlords for these years.[2] The 1909 estimate thus derived was projected to 1899 on the basis of the value of farm products for the respective years, as estimated by the Department of Agriculture.[3]

MINING AND QUARRYING

Net rents and royalties for this industry represent the sum of separate estimates made for oil and gas wells, coal-mining and metal-mining industries, for the respective years.

Oil and Gas Wells, Coal Mining

Estimates of net rents and royalties for these industries were obtained by projecting the 1929 estimates to 1899 on the basis of data on the volume of crude petroleum production and coal production respectively.[4]

Metal Mining

The 1929 estimate of net rents and royalties for this industry was projected to 1899 on the basis of data on the value of metal products.[5]

MANUFACTURING

Net rents and royalties, as estimated for 1929 in manufacturing, were assumed for 1904, 1909 and 1919 to be approximately one-

[1] "Income from Farm Production," 1935, p. 10.

[2] "National Income and Its Purchasing Power," op. cit., p. 308.

[3] "Statistical Abstract of the United States, 1931," p. 699.

[4] The sources are: "Minerals Yearbook, 1937," p. 1009; "Census of Manufactures, 1929," Table 7, p. 257; "Mineral Resources, 1929," Part I, p. A 7.

[5] Idem.

half of the amount reported as factory rent in the 1909 and 1919 Censuses of Manufactures.

Estimates of net rents and royalties for the other years were derived as follows: the amounts reported as value added by manufacture were taken from the 1929 Census of Manufactures for each census year from 1899 to 1929 inclusive. Estimates for the years 1910–1914 and 1920–1937 were obtained by a straight line interpolation between the census figures. Estimates of the value added by manufacture for 1899–1909 and 1915–1919 were obtained by apportioning the actual difference between the census years on the basis of a percentage distribution of the actual change, from year to year, of the Bureau of Labor Statistics index of wholesale prices for the corresponding periods.

Ratios of the estimated net rents and royalties to the value added by manufacture were then computed for 1904, 1909, 1919 and 1929 and interpolated for the other years. The resulting ratios were applied to the annual estimates of value added by manufacture to arrive at estimates of net rents and royalties from 1904 to 1929 inclusive.

The 1904 estimate of net rents and royalties thus derived was projected to 1899 on the basis of the estimates for the value added by manufacture for the respective years.

TRANSPORTATION, COMMUNICATION, ELECTRIC LIGHT AND
POWER AND GAS, AND CONSTRUCTION

Because of a lack of adequate data, it was impossible to make direct estimates of this type of income for these industries. Rough estimates based on sample data indicating probable trends were obtained as follows:

Transportation

The 1929 estimate was projected to 1908 on the basis of the results obtained by deducting rents received from rents paid as reported annually in the "Statistics of Railways."

Electric Light and Power and Gas

The 1929 estimate of net rents and royalties was projected to 1908 on the basis of data on the total volume of electricity produced annually from 1919 to 1929, and on census data for 1902 and 1912.[1]

[1] "Statistical Abstract of the United States, 1936," p. 348.

Estimates of the total volume of electricity produced for the other years were obtained by a straight-line interpolation of the census figures and the 1919 estimate.

Communication

The 1929 estimate of net rents and royalties was projected to 1909 on the basis of the trend of estimated net rents and royalties in electric light and power and gas.

Construction

Estimates of net rents and royalties in construction for the years prior to 1929 were arrived at by projecting the 1929 estimate on the basis of data on the volume of actual construction installation for the respective years.[1]

TRADE

The 1929 estimate of net rents and royalties was projected to 1899 on the basis of the trend of the estimates of entrepreneurial income for the respective years.

SERVICE

Estimates of net rents and royalties in the service industry from 1899 to 1929 were obtained by projecting the 1929 estimate on the basis of the trend of salaries and wages for this industry.

FINANCE AND MISCELLANEOUS

Estimates of net rents and royalties from 1899 to 1929 for the finance and miscellaneous classifications were obtained by projecting the 1929 estimates on the basis of the trend of the sum of the estimates of the foregoing industries.

6. Other Accountable Income Items

INTEREST ON OWNED HOMES

The 1929 estimate of interest on owned homes was projected to 1899 on the basis of Mr. Kuvin's estimates of interest charges on non-farm mortgages for the respective years.[2]

---

[1] United States Department of Commerce, "Survey of Current Business, Annual Supplement, 1931," p. 190.

[2] Kuvin, *op. cit.*, p. 42.

NET RESIDENTIAL RENT

Net residential rent includes estimates of net rent on non-farm and farm homes, derived separately, from 1899 to 1929.

Estimates of net rent on non-farm homes were obtained by projecting the 1929 estimate to 1909 on the basis of the trend of Dr. Leven's estimates of residential rent for the respective years.[1] The 1909 estimate thus secured was projected to 1899 on the basis of estimates of net rent derived as follows: the number of rented non-farm dwellings was taken from the 1910 Census of Population for 1909, and an estimate of the number of rented non-farm dwellings made for 1899 on the basis of data on the total number of non-farm dwellings and the percentage of non-farm dwellings rented, obtained from the same source. Intercensal estimates of the number of non-farm rented dwellings were obtained by a straight-line interpolation between the census figures.

The annual estimates of the number of non-farm rented dwellings thus derived were multiplied by an index of residential rents, obtained for the respective years by reading the data from the curve of the chart published in *The Real Estate Analyst* of January, 1938, pp. 864ff.

Estimates of net rent on farm dwellings from 1909 to 1929 were obtained by projecting the 1929 estimate on the basis of the same trend used in estimating net rents and royalties in agriculture for the respective years. The 1909 estimate thus derived was projected to 1899 on the basis of estimates of net rent on farm dwellings obtained in the same manner as described for non-farm dwellings for the respective years.

PENSIONS AND COMPENSATION FOR INJURIES

Private

Estimates of pensions paid in private industry for 1927 and 1928 were obtained as described for the year 1929.

Estimates of compensation payments for 1927 and 1928 were secured by projecting the 1929 estimate on the basis of the estimated total salaries and wages in private industry.

The separate estimates were added for 1927 and for 1928. The combined estimate for 1927 was then projected to 1909 on the basis of the results obtained by deducting government pensions and com-

[1] Leven, *op. cit.*, p. 153.

pensation payments from total pensions and compensation payments as estimated by Dr. King for the respective years.[1]   The 1909 estimate thus secured was projected to 1899 on the basis of the trend of the sum of the estimated salaries and wages in mining, manufacturing and transportation.

Public

Estimates of government pensions and compensation payments for 1927 and 1928 were derived in the same manner as the 1929 estimates.   The 1927 estimate of total government pensions and compensation payments was then projected to 1909 on the basis of Dr. King's estimates for 1909–1929.[2]   The 1909 estimate, thus derived, was projected to 1899 on the basis of the amounts expended for war service pensions for the respective years.[3]

PRIVATE DIRECT RELIEF PAYMENTS

All data utilized for these estimates were obtained from publications of, and correspondence with, The John Price Jones Corporation, New York.

The 1929 estimate of private direct relief was projected to 1921 on the basis of data on the amounts of bequests to educational, philanthropic, religious and charitable institutions for each year.[4] The 1921 estimate was then projected to 1910 on the basis of the trend of the sum of the number of donations to Children's Aid Societies and the number of contributions to Associations for Improving the Condition of the Poor, obtained by correspondence, for the respective years. The 1910 estimate of the amount of donations to philanthropy, thus secured, was assumed constant for the years 1899–1910 inclusive.

B. NATIONAL INCOME, CENSUS YEARS, 1799–1899

In the foregoing description of methods, one phrase, "the 1929 figure was projected to 1899 on the basis of an index . . .", has recurred time and again.   Some explanation of the method of projection used is therefore in order.

[1] "National Income and Its Purchasing Power," *op. cit.*, pp. 74, 369.

[2] *Idem.*

[3] "Statistical Abstract of the United States, 1934," p. 151.

[4] The John Price Jones Corporation, New York, "America Gives Away $2,219,700,000 in a Year."

Many of the sources used in making the estimates for 1929 were not available for earlier years. In order to obtain comparable totals for the various years the procedure generally adopted has been to make the best estimate possible for 1929 and preceding years on the basis of source material that is comparable throughout the period. The estimate for each item for each year has therefore been expressed as a percentage of the comparable estimate for 1929. Finally, each of these percentages has been applied to a second 1929 estimate based on all available data, and the result has been used as the final estimate for the year which that particular percentage represented. For example, entrepreneurial income in a certain industry in 1911 may have been exactly 50% of the figure estimated for 1929 on the basis of comparable source material. The most dependable figure for 1929, which was based on all data available for that year, whether or not comparable with available figures for earlier years, was then multiplied by 50% to give the estimated entrepreneurial income for 1911.

With a single relatively unimportant exception,[1] this principle has been applied throughout in estimating the national income in the nineteenth century. The most accurate estimates that could be constructed of the income produced in each industrial group in each census year were used to project the final estimates for 1899[2] back over the preceding 100 years. The following sections take up the sources and methods used in constructing these index series.

An understanding of the methods will be made easier by an explanation of certain terms which appear frequently in the description. When a series is "linked" or "tied" to an estimate for a particular year, or when such an estimate is "projected," "extended," or "carried back," on a series, what is done is exactly the same as the process described above in connection with the carrying back of the 1929 estimates through the year 1899. The assumption involved is that the fluctuations in the series on which an estimate is carried back are the same in direction and in relative size as the fluctuations in the figure the estimate of which is carried back.

When a series is "inflated," it is adjusted so as to reflect price changes. For example, we might have a series representing the number of bushels of oats produced in each census year. In order to estimate income produced by growers of oats, the procedure

---

[1] The fishing industry.

[2] These 1899 estimates were made by use of the sources and methods described in the preceding section of this Appendix.

would be to "inflate" this series of physical quantities by multiplying the quantity given for each year by an index number showing
the price of oats in that year as related to the price of oats in some
"base" year. Suppose that between 1810 and 1890 the production
of oats doubled in physical volume. Suppose further that an index
of the price of oats showed that in 1810 the price was 175% of the
price in the base year, while in 1890 the index showed a price only
87.5% of that in the base year. The production figure for 1810
would be multiplied by 175%; the production figure for 1890 would
be multiplied by 87.5%. The inflated index would show that the
total real income produced by growers of oats was the same in
1810 as in 1890, as would in fact have been the case. In a few
cases a series of values was "deflated" instead of being inflated.
The procedure here was just the reverse; the value series was
divided by price index numbers, so that the effect of price changes
on the total value produced was eliminated.

Three sorts of price indexes were used in making these income
estimates. To indicate wholesale prices, the Warren-Pearson wholesale price index using variable group weight was selected. This
index has been published in a volume entitled "Wholesale Prices
for 213 Years, 1720 to 1932," by Cornell University (1932). The
Conference Board's Cost of Living Index was correlated with this
wholesale price index and extended back through 1799 on the basis
of the apparent relationship between the two indexes. The third
price index used in the study, the "General Price Level," was
based on that constructed by Mr. Carl Snyder of the New York
Federal Reserve Bank, which was extended from 1880 back to 1799
by the same method employed in projecting the Cost of Living
Index back to that date.

In making the estimates for 1899 and later years, data originally
reported on a fiscal year basis were converted to apply to calendar
years by computing averages of two consecutive fiscal years. This
method is not practicable where the basic data are collected only at
ten-year intervals. Consequently, the estimates made for the
earlier years, that is, between 1799 and 1889, inclusive, apply to no
specific year but to a twelve months' period beginning and ending
within the two years beginning on January 1 of the year indicated.
For example, the totals for 1799 for each industry represent the
income realized during a twelve-months' period beginning some
time after January 1, 1799 and ending some time before January 1,
1801.

AGRICULTURE

Estimates of income from agriculture for the second half of the nineteenth century were based directly on census figures, unchanged save for the deduction of the value of domestic manufactures where this was reported separately. The Census of 1860 reported production largely in terms of physical quantities, and the valuation of Michael Mulhall[1] was used in the manner explained below to estimate the value of reported production in that year.

For the year 1860, an estimate was made by interpolating on the curve of agricultural production as reported by the censuses the rate of change shown by Mulhall for the aggregate value of grain, cotton, hay, potatoes, tobacco, vegetables and fruit, meat and tallow, dairy products, eggs and poultry, wool and hides, etc.

The estimates for the first half of the century are based on a weighted composite index, the components of which purport to show the value of each class of farm products. Total value of agricultural production in 1870 was taken as the base for the index, the components being weighted roughly according to the relative value of the various groups of products in 1850. The system used in weighting was to assign to each component series a weight corresponding to the value of all products the recorded production of which showed the same trend as did the component.

The values used in constructing the index were taken largely from Mulhall. Component series included and weights used are as follows:

Series	Unit	Weight
I. *Production*		
A Grain	bushel	26.1
B Cotton	pound	7.6
C Tobacco	"	20.8
II. *Domestic consumption*		
D Grain	bushel	4.3
E Cotton	pound	0.4
F Tobacco	"	0.5
III. *Miscellaneous*		
G Capital invested in agriculture[2]	dollars	20.9
H Population of United States	person	6.0
IV. *Compound series*		
ABC total value of grain, cotton, and tobacco produced	1910–14 dollars	3.5
BC total value of cotton and tobacco produced	1910–14 dollars	0.3
DEF total value of grain, cotton, and tobacco consumed	1910–14 dollars	9.6

[1] See Michael Mulhall, "The Dictionary of Statistics," London, 1903.

[2] See below.

This composite index was inflated by using the Warren-Pearson index of wholesale prices of farm products. Estimates of the total value of farm production for the census years 1800 through 1840 were then made on the basis of the relationship shown by the index between 1870 and the earlier years.

As a result of these methods a series was obtained showing the estimated value of agricultural production in each census year from 1800 through 1900. The next step was to subtract allowances for seed, fertilizer and depreciation. The value of farm implements and machinery on farms was obtained from the census reports for 1850 and succeeding years. Mulhall[1] published estimates of the value of agricultural capital for 1810 and 1840–80 inclusive. The figure for implements and machinery was carried back to 1810 on the basis of these estimates, and values for 1800, 1820 and 1830 were obtained by reading from the smoothed curve. Of the value of implements and machinery, thus estimated, 6% was assumed to be a fair allowance for depreciation. For cost of seed, a deduction was made of 3% of the value of total agricultural production, or about 4.7% of the value of crops.[2] In order to determine the amount to be deducted for cost of fertilizer, the value of artificial fertilizer manufactured in 1890 and 1900, as reported by the census, was deflated by use of a price index. A constant rate of increase in the quantity produced was assumed for 1850–1900. Quantities estimated on this basis for the earlier years were inflated by the price index, and taken as a final deduction from total value produced on farms.

These deductions having been made, the series of values of net production was linked to the figure computed by the Conference Board for farm income in 1899.

MANUFACTURING

In estimating income produced in the manufacturing industry, the general plan was to deduct from total value of output the cost of raw materials, taxes, repairs, and losses by fire, flood, etc. Census data as to output, raw materials and capital were available for all census years except 1800 and 1830, when no inquiry was made into the state of manufacturing industry, and 1810, when only output figures were gathered. Taxes, repairs and losses of

[1] Mulhall, *op. cit.*, p. 46.

[2] United States Department of Agriculture, "Yearbook of Agriculture, 1935," Washington, D. C., p. 675. Ratio of seed cost to crop sales.

types usually covered by insurance were assumed to average 2.2%[1] of the capital investment annually.

Important adjustments were necessary in most of this census material, both to render the figures comparable from year to year and to allow for under-reporting and omissions.

The major respects in which the several censuses differed in scope, and the adjustments made on this account, were as follows:

> *1850* and *1860:* Included mining and fishing under the head of manufacturing. The capital, raw materials and output figures reported for these industries were deducted from the corresponding totals reported for manufacturing.

> *1870:* Included parts of mining and fishing under Manufactures. The capital, output and raw materials assigned to these parts were deducted from the corresponding totals for manufacturing.

The cost of raw materials and miscellaneous expenses (2.2% of capital) were now deducted from the total value of output for each year to obtain a net product. To this was added the value of "family manufacturing" for the years before 1880, this item having been reported in the censuses of Agriculture rather than of Manufactures for these years. The net products computed from the Censuses of Manufactures for illuminating gas in the years 1850–1900, and for electric power production in the years 1880–1890, were deducted from the net value of factory and family manufacturing. The resulting series for net manufacturing product was used as an index of income in manufacturing, the estimates for 1899 being projected back to 1849–1850 on this basis.

Before the adjustments described above were made, the census material for the years 1850, 1860 and 1870 was corrected for under-reporting. The 1860 and 1870 totals finally used were those estimated by General Francis A. Walker, Superintendent of the Census in 1870, from a comparison of the reports of the Census of Manufactures and of the Census of Occupations. His assumption was that the reasonable excess of persons reporting as gainfully occupied over the number reported as actually employed ranged from 6% to 16%.[2]

---

[1] On the basis of data published in the "Census of 1890" for a sample group of industries having about 13% of the total manufacturing capital.

[2] See the "Ninth Census of the United States, 1870," Vol. III, pp. 373–379: "Statistics of Wealth and Industry of the United States."

The same method, simplified in accordance with the limited nature of the data available, was used in adjusting the census reports for 1820, 1840 and 1850. Omissions in 1840 were estimated under the assumption that 16% of the gainful workers in manufacturing industry were for one reason or another unemployed, and that the ratio of the number of gainful workers remaining unaccounted for in the production tables of the census to the total number reported as employed represented the proportion of omitted to reported production. No suitable data on occupations being available for 1850, straight line interpolation between the percentages of omission in 1840 and 1860 was used to estimate the extent of omissions in 1850.

The series used as an index of income in manufacturing for 1839–1840 and earlier years was of the same general nature as that employed for the second half of the century. It was considered that neither the figures reported as total capital investment nor the 1890 ratio of capital to miscellaneous expenses could safely be used; consequently, cost of materials was the only deduction made from total value of output. The net value of production in 1830 was interpolated on a smooth curve, and the value for 1800 was extrapolated on the same curve.

MINING AND TRANSPORTATION

Conference Board estimates for 1899 of income from mining and quarrying and from transportation and communication were projected back through 1849–1850 on the basis of Dr. King's figures for income in these industries.[1] The series on which are based estimates for the years 1799–1850 for these industries are described below.

Mining and Quarrying

Total value of mining production in 1850 was taken from the census and adjusted for omissions by use of the same ratio employed for raising manufacturing production in that year.[2] Total mining production in 1840 was estimated from the adjusted 1850 figures by use of the ratio of the value of iron, gold, coal, salt and quarry products mined in 1840 to the value of these in 1850. Production

---

[1] King, "Wealth and Income of the People of the United States," New York, 1919, p. 138; also unpublished material.

[2] See Manufacturing, above.

from mines in 1820 was estimated by raising the values reported to the census for manufacturing and mining production so as to include an average output for 84% of the number of persons reporting manufacturing or mining as their occupation.[1] Income from mining in 1810 was calculated on the assumption that the share of this industry in the value of total manufacturing and mining production was the same as in 1820.

A smooth curve was next fitted to these estimates, covering the years 1810, 1820, 1840 and 1850.

This curve was extended to 1799–1800, and readings taken at 1800 and at 1830. These readings were used with the above estimates to form an index series on which the original estimate for 1850 was carried back to 1799–1800.

Transportation and Communication

From unpublished estimates made by Dr. King, it was possible to break down his figure for transportation in 1850 into two parts, water and land. These values respectively were used as weights in a composite index including an inflated series of domestic shipping tonnage engaged in trade[2] and a series of the annual values of the total commercial movement (see Commerce). This composite index was employed as a basis on which to project the 1849 estimate back through 1799–1800.

LIGHT AND POWER

The series representing income from the light and power industry was based on census data for 1849–1850 and succeeding years. Figures for capital, cost of raw materials, and output of illuminating gas and electric power were treated as were the corresponding figures for the manufacturing industry (see Manufacturing) to obtain estimates of net income produced.

No figures for the gas industry were reported in the census of 1860 or in that of 1880. Data on the electric power industry were not reported prior to 1880. The 1880 census figures for the latter were carried back through 1850 on the basis of estimates by Dr. King for private electric companies.[3] The missing figures in the gas

---

[1] See Manufacturing, above.

[2] Estimated from data published in J. D. B. De Bow, "Compendium of the Seventh Census," Washington, D. C., 1854, p. 191, and in the "Statistical Abstract of the United States, 1912," p. 784.

[3] "Wealth and Income," op. cit., pp. 260–263.

industry series were estimated from smoothed curves drawn on a semi-logarithmic scale.

The series of net income figures thus derived was extended back through 1829–1830, consideration being given to the early history of the use of illuminating gas in this country. The estimates of income from electric light and power and gas for 1899 were projected back through 1829–1830 on the basis of this extended series.

COMMERCE

Estimates of income in commerce for the second half of the nineteenth century are based on the number of persons reported to the census as pursuing specified commercial occupations in these years. This series was inflated by use of an index of the general level of wholesale prices, and the estimate of income in commerce previously prepared for 1899 was carried back through 1849–1850 on the inflated series.

The total thus obtained for 1849–1850 was carried back through 1799–1800 on a composite index of the annual commercial movement constructed as follows: From data and estimates from the Compendium of the Sixth Census[1] and elsewhere, the total value of the commerce of the country as a whole in 1850 was broken down into four divisions. These were western river, Great Lakes, foreign, and coastwise and overland trade. An index was prepared for each division. The value of western river commerce was carried back on a series of the value of exports from the state of Louisiana.[2] The value of Great Lakes trade was projected back through 1820 on the basis of the shipping tonnage in the trade on the Lakes,[3] and extended back through 1800 on the assumption of a constant rate of increase. The value of coastwise and overland commerce was carried back through 1800 on an inflated series of shipping tonnage in the coastwise trade. The figures for total foreign trade were taken directly from the Statistical Abstract.[4] These estimates of the value of commercial movement were then combined to form the index on which the 1850 figure for income in commerce was carried back through 1800.

[1] *Op. cit.*, p. 189.

[2] *Ibid.*, p. 187. Extended from 1810 back to 1800 on assumption of a constant rate of increase.

[3] Inflated by use of wholesale price index.

[4] United States Bureau of Foreign and Domestic Commerce, "Statistical Abstract of the United States, 1908," pp. 670–671.

CONSTRUCTION

The series used to indicate changes in income from building construction during the nineteenth century consisted of two parts. The section extending from 1850 through 1899 was constructed from rough estimates of total wages earned in the industry. These were derived from the census reports of the number of persons in various building trades, with average real wage rates in each trade over the period.

The section of the index covering the years 1800–1850 was a composite of two series, first, the tonnage of American vessels built annually[1] and, second, the annual increase in the population of the country. These were weighted according to the value respectively of ships and of houses reported built during the census year 1840, and the composite series was linked to the 1850 figure for total wages earned.

The whole series, 1800–1899, was finally inflated by use of a wholesale price index and used as a basis on which to project back through 1799–1800 the estimates of income in building construction for 1899.

GOVERNMENT

The series used to indicate the amount of income from government between 1860 and 1899 consisted of the estimates of total per capita taxes prepared by Dr. King.[2] To obtain figures for the years 1800–1850, this series was deflated and the result charted as a smooth curve. An estimate of the total per capita cost of government made by the United States Secretary of State in 1832[3] was deflated and incorporated in the curve, as was an estimate for 1850 made by averaging Dr. King's figure for 1850 with an amount computed by J. D. B. De Bow[4] from incomplete census returns for that year. By extrapolation on the curve, the per capita real cost of government was estimated for 1800, 1810, 1820 and 1830. A reading from the curve was also taken for 1840, while the average above referred to was accepted for 1850. The whole series was now reflated and per capita taxes for each year multiplied by the population returned by the census for that year. The result was used to

---

[1] "Statistical Abstract of the United States, 1912," p. 784.

[2] "Wealth and Income," *op. cit.*, p. 143.

[3] "Compendium of the Seventh Census," *op. cit.*, p. 190.

[4] *Idem.*

project back to 1800 the estimate for total income in government for 1899.

SERVICE

The estimate of total national income from the service industry in 1899 was carried back through 1849–1850 on the basis of the number of individuals in service occupations, and projected to 1799–1800 on an index of the urban population of the country.

The series consisting of the number reported to each census after 1840 as engaged in service was inflated by use of a price index. The total number of inhabitants in twenty-three leading cities at each census from 1800 through 1850 was likewise inflated, and the result linked to the occupations series at 1850. The estimate for 1899 was carried back to 1799–1800 on the index thus derived.

MISCELLANEOUS PRODUCTION

The Conference Board income estimates for 1899 and succeeding years do not include fishing as a distinct industry. Finance, however, is classified separately. The 1899 estimate of income in finance was therefore added to the total of the miscellaneous group for that year. Dr. King's estimate[1] of income from fishing was deducted from total miscellaneous production. With these adjustments, the 1899 figure for miscellaneous industries was carried back through 1799–1800 on an index of all other realized production income.

Dr. King's estimates of income from fishing have been accepted in toto for the years 1850–1900. An inflated series of the shipping tonnage[2] in the whale, cod, and mackerel fisheries was used to carry these income estimates back to 1799–1800.

C. OTHER ACCOUNTABLE INCOME ITEMS, 1799–1889

SECTION 1: UNDERLYING ESTIMATES

A considerable part of the material used in making the estimates described below was of necessity likewise based on estimates. In this category fall the classifying of homes as farm or non-farm, as well as the apportionment of these groups between tenure classes.

---

[1] "Wealth and Income," *op. cit.*, p. 138.

[2] Estimated from data in the "Compendium of the Seventh Census," *op. cit.*, p. 191, and the Statistical Abstract for 1912, *op. cit.*, p. 784.

The rent indexes for both farm and non-farm homes and the series of ratios of debt to value with regard to non-farm real estate were also estimated. These problems will be taken up in order.

In order to determine the total number of homes in each census year, the average family size was read from a curve incorporating census data for 1790 and for the years after 1850. The total population figure at each census was then divided by the average size of family. Census figures for the number of farm families for 1890 and subsequent years and for the number of farms at each enumeration from 1850 through 1880 were subtracted from the total number of families. In this way estimates of the number of farm and of non-farm families for 1850 and succeeding years were obtained. Each of these two series was next charted on a semilogarithmic scale and the trends projected back to 1800. These projected trend lines were adjusted upward and downward until the sum of the readings from the two smooth curves for each census year equalled the estimated total number of all families in that year, the degree of curvature in the two lines being approximately equal. The readings taken were assumed to represent the approximate distribution of the population between farm and non-farm families.

The next problem was to obtain tenancy ratios for each of these classes. A rough correlation was found, using census data for the years 1880–1930, between farm tenancy and the valuation per acre of agricultural land and buildings. A smooth curve was drawn through the plotted points from the latter series,[1] and readings taken for 1800, 1820, 1830 and 1840. Readings from the line of relationship between tenancy and valuation in the census years 1880–1930 were then taken to determine the tenancy ratio corresponding to the value of farms per acre in each census year before 1880. The ratios thus obtained for 1799–1880, with the census ratios for 1880–1900, were applied to the estimated number of farm homes in the respective years. The resulting series was accepted as the number of rented farm homes, 1799–1900.

The tenancy ratios for non-farm homes were estimated by a similar procedure. It was assumed that a relationship existed between non-farm tenancy and the average price of a home. The closest approximation to this latter figure obtainable was the value per non-farm family of all non-farm real estate. The census figure for total value of all property for 1900 was carried back through

---

[1] Based on census figures after 1840, and Mulhall's estimates for 1810.

1860 on the basis of total assessed value of real property, and through 1850 on the basis of the changes in the true value of all property. The resulting series was divided by the estimated number of non-farm families to give the requisite value per family for the years 1850–1900. In order to estimate the comparable values for 1800–1840, this series was deflated by a rough index of the cost of living, charted on a semi-logarithmic scale, and a smooth curve drawn through all known points and extended back to 1800. Readings from this curve were deflated and used as values of non-farm real estate per non-farm family, 1800–1840.

It was felt that the twentieth century development of new methods of transportation had altered the old relationship between tenancy and land values. Instead of attempting to estimate tenancy ratios on the basis of the relationship prevailing after 1900, therefore, it was arbitrarily assumed that a non-farm tenancy ratio of 5% existed in 1800. This percentage was plotted against the average value of non-farm real estate per non-farm family in that year. The tenancy ratios published in the census for 1890 and 1900 were likewise plotted against the value of such real estate per family. A regular curve was drawn through these three points, and the tenancy ratio corresponding to the estimated value of real estate per family in each census year was read off and recorded. These ratios were applied to the corresponding totals for number of non-farm families, to obtain the number of non-farm homes rented in each year.[1]

No satisfactory index of rents was available for census years prior to 1870. That published by the Real Estate Analysts, Inc., in *The Real Estate Analyst* in 1938,[2] was correlated roughly with the cost-of-living index for the years 1870–1879, and extended back to 1799–1800. The index number for each census year was then multiplied by the value per non-farm family of non-farm real estate in that year. The resulting series showed the trend of land values and the cyclical fluctuations of the cost of living. This series was used as an index of non-farm residential rents.

The Real Estate Analyst index of residential rents was extended back from 1870 to 1799–1800 on the series of values per acre of farm real estate, and used as an index of the farm home rent level.

The debt-value ratio used in estimating the amounts of interest

---

[1] These were subtracted from total non-farm homes to give the number of owned non-farm homes for which interest payments were estimated. See below.

[2] *Op. cit.*, p. 865.

on owned homes was derived from the ratios published by the Conference Board[1] for 1900, 1904, 1912, 1922 and 1929. This series was charted on a semi-logarithmic scale. A smooth curve was drawn, representing the trend of the ratios, and was extended back to 1799–1800. Readings from this curve for the census years of the nineteenth century were used as the debt-value ratios.

SECTION 2: FINAL ESTIMATES

Interest on Owned Homes:

To obtain estimates for the amount of interest on owned homes, the procedure was as follows: For each census year during the period the product of three factors was computed:[2] value of all non-farm real estate and improvements per non-farm family, the ratio of mortgage debt encumbrance to value of non-farm real estate, and the number of owned non-farm homes. The resulting series was used as an index on which to project back to 1799–1800 the Conference Board estimate for 1900 of interest on owned homes.[3]

Private Pensions and Compensation for Injuries:

Conference Board estimates[2] of the value of this item for 1899–1938 were charted on a semi-logarithmic scale. A trend line was fitted to the plotted points and projected back and downward to the $500,000 level. Readings taken from this curve for the census years 1859–1890 are presented as the final estimates of the value of this item.

Private Direct Relief:

A series representing physical production in manufacturing, 1799–1900, was derived by deflating the dollar amounts of manufacturing income with an index of the prices of manufactured products.[4] To the series so obtained was fitted a trend line, from which values were read off for each census year. The percentage deviation of the actual production was next computed.

It was assumed that relief payments would vary inversely to

---

[1] Kuvin, *op. cit.*, pp. 63ff. Ratio of accountable non-farm mortgage debt to the value of non-farm real property.

[2] See above, Section 1, for sources.   [3] Unpublished.

[4] Derived from Warren-Pearson's group indexes, in "Wholesale Prices for 213 Years," *op. cit.*

manufacturing production in the short run, but would in the long run increase proportionately with the increasing importance of manufacturing industry as a source of national income. Therefore, the positive deviations of physical production from trend were expressed as negative percentages, and vice versa. These percentages were next applied to values read from the trend line of income produced in manufacturing. In effect, then, the trend of these relief estimates is the trend of manufacturing income; the cyclical movements are equal in degree but opposite in direction to the fluctuations in physical volume of manufacturing production.

Net Rent on Non-farm Homes:

These figures were obtained by use of two separate series. The number of rented non-farm homes was calculated for each census year by deducting from the number of all homes an estimate of the number of farm homes,[1] and applying to the result a percentage ratio[1] of non-farm rented to all non-farm homes. The result was multiplied by an index number[1] representing the level of non-farm residential rents. The Conference Board estimate[2] of net rent on non-farm homes in 1900 was projected back to 1799–1800 on the basis of this final series.

Net Rent on Farm Homes:

A corresponding procedure was adopted for farm homes, the number rented being obtained by use of a tenancy ratio,[1] then multiplied by the index of the farm rent level,[1] and finally tied to the Conference Board estimate[1] of net rent on farm homes for 1900.

Government Pensions and Compensation for Injuries:

The Conference Board estimate[2] of the value of this item was carried back to 1799–1800 on the assumption that these payments maintained a constant proportional relationship to the pension disbursements[3] of the Federal Government.

[1] See above, Section 1, for sources and methods of deriving this series.
[2] Unpublished.
[3] United States Bureau of Foreign and Domestic Commerce, "Statistical Abstract of the United States, 1922," p. 650.

AMERICA IN TWO CENTURIES:
An Inventory

An Arno Press Collection

American Association of Museums. **A Statistical Survey of Museums in the United States and Canada.** 1965

Andrews, Israel D. **On the Trade and Commerce of the British North American Colonies, and Upon the Trade of the Great Lakes and Rivers.** 1853

Audit Bureau of Circulations. **Scientific Space Selection.** 1921

Austin, E. L. and Odell Hauser. **The Sesqui-Centennial International Exposition.** 1929

Barnett, James H. **The American Christmas.** 1954

Barton, L| eslie | M. **A Study of 81 Principal American Markets.** 1925

Bennitt, Mark, comp. **History of the Louisiana Purchase Exposition.** 1905

Bowen, Eli. **The United States Post-Office Guide.** 1851

Bureau of Applied Social Research, Columbia University. **The People Look at Radio.** 1946

Burlingame, Roger. **Engines of Democracy:** Inventions and Society in Mature America. 1940

Burlingame, Roger. **March of the Iron Men:** A Social History of Union Through Invention. 1938

Burnham, W. Dean. **Presidential Ballots, 1836-1892.** 1955

Cochrane, Rexmond C. **Measures for Progress:** A History of the National Bureau of Standards. 1966

Cohn, David L. **The Good Old Days.** 1940

Cozens, Frederick W. and Florence Scovil Stumpf. **Sports in American Life.** 1953

Day, Edmund E. and Woodlief Thomas. **The Growth of Manufactures, 1899 to 1923.** 1928

Edwards, Richard Henry. **Popular Amusements.** 1915

Evans, Charles H., comp. **Exports, Domestic and Foreign, From the American Colonies to Great Britain, From 1697 to 1789, Inclusive;** Exports, Domestic, From the U.S. to All Countries, From 1789 to 1883, Inclusive. 1884

Federal Reserve System, Board of Governors. **All-Bank Statistics, United States, 1896-1955.** 1959

Flexner, Abraham. **Funds and Foundations:** Their Policies, Past and Present. 1952

Flint, Henry M. **The Railroads of the United States.** 1868

Folger, John K. and Charles B. Nam. **Education of the American Population.** 1967

Handel, Leo A. **Hollywood Looks At Its Audience:** A Report of Film Audience Research. 1950

Harlow, Alvin F. **Old Waybills:** The Romance of the Express Companies. 1934

Harrison, Shelby M. **Social Conditions in an American City:** A Summary of the Findings of the Springfield Survey. 1920

Homans, J. Smith, comp. **An Historical and Statistical Account of the Foreign Commerce of the United States.** 1857

Ingram, J. S. **The Centennial Exposition.** 1876

Institute of American Meat Packers and the School of Commerce and Administration of the University of Chicago. **The Packing Industry:** A Series of Lectures. 1924

Leech, D[aniel] D. T[ompkins]. **The Post Office Department of the United States of America.** 1879

Leggett, M. D., comp. **Subject-Matter Index of Patents for Inventions Issued by the United States Patent Office From 1790 to 1873, Inclusive.** 1874. Three vols.

Magazine Marketing Service. **M.M.S. County Buying Power Index.** 1942

Martin, Robert F. **National Income in the United States, 1799-1938.** 1939

McCullough, Edo. **World's Fair Midways.** 1966

Melish, John. **Surveys for Travellers, Emigrants and Others.** 1976

National Advertising Company. **America's Advertisers.** 1893

Peters, Harry T. **America On Stone:** The Other Printmakers to the American People. 1931

Peters, Harry T. **California On Stone.** 1935

Peters, Harry T. **Currier & Ives:** Printmakers to the American People. 1929/1931. Two vols.

Pownall, T[homas]. **A Topographical Description of the Dominions of the United States of America.** Edited by Lois Mulkearn. 1949

Reed, Alfred Zantzinger. **Present-Day Law Schools in the United States and Canada.** 1928

Reed, Alfred Zantzinger. **Training for the Public Profession of the Law.** 1921

Rogers, Meyric R. **American Interior Design.** 1947

Romaine, Lawrence B. **A Guide to American Trade Catalogs, 1744-1900.** 1960

Scammon, Richard M., comp. **America at the Polls:** A Handbook of American Presidential Election Statistics, 1920-1964. 1965

Smillie, Wilson G. **Public Health:** Its Promise for the Future. 1955

Thompson, Warren S. **Population: The Growth of Metropolitan Districts in the United States, 1900-1940.** 1947

Thorndike, E[dward] L. **Your City.** 1939

Truman, Ben[jamin] C. **History of the World's Fair.** 1893

U.S. Bureau of the Census, Department of Commerce. **Housing Construction Statistics: 1889 to 1964.** 1966

U.S. Census Office (12th Census). **Street and Electric Railways.** 1903

Urban Statistical Surveys. 1976

Wayland, Sloan and Edmund de S. Brunner. **The Educational Characteristics of the American People.** 1958

Woytinsky, W. S. **Employment and Wages in the United States.** 1953

U.S. Census Office (1st Census, 1790). **Return of the Whole Number of Persons Within the Several Districts of the United States.** 1802

U.S. Census Office (2nd Census, 1800). **Return of the Whole Number of Persons Within the Several Districts of the United States.** 1802

U.S. Census Office (3rd Census, 1810). **Aggregate Amount of Each Description of Persons Within the United States of America.** 1811

U.S. Census Office (4th Census, 1820). **Census for 1820.** 1821

U.S. Census Office (5th Census, 1830). **Abstract of the Returns of the Fifth Census.** 1832

U.S. Census Office (6th Census, 1840). **Compendium of the Enumeration of the Inhabitants and Statistics of the United States.** 1841

U.S. Census Office (7th Census, 1850). **The Seventh Census of the United States.** 1853

U.S. Census Office (8th Census, 1860). **Statistics of the United States in 1860.** 1866

U.S. Census Office (9th Census, 1870). **A Compendium of the Ninth Census.** 1872

U.S. Census Office (10th Census, 1880). **Compendium of the Tenth Census.** Parts I and II. 1883. Two vols.

U.S. Census Office (11th Census, 1890). **Abstract of the Eleventh Census.** 1894

U.S. Bureau of the Census (12th Census, 1900). **Abstract of the Twelfth Census of the United States.** 1904

U.S. Bureau of the Census (13th Census, 1910). **Thirteenth Census of the United States: Abstract of the Census.** 1913

U.S. Bureau of the Census (14th Census, 1920). **Abstract of the Fourteenth Census of the United States.** 1923

U.S. Bureau of the Census (15th Census, 1930). **Fifteenth Census of the United States: Abstract of the Census.** 1933

U.S. Bureau of the Census (16th Census, 1940). **Sixteenth Census of the United States: United States Summary.** 1943

U.S. Bureau of the Census (17th Census, 1950). **A Report of the Seventeenth Decennial Census of the United States: United States Summary.** 1953

U.S. Bureau of the Census (18th Census, 1960). **The Eighteenth Decennial Census of the United States: United States Summary.** 1964

U.S. Bureau of the Census (19th Census, 1970). **1970 Census of Population: United States Summary.** 1973. Two vols.